WARTIME HOUSEWIFE

WARTIME HOUSEWIFE

A No-Nonsense Handbook
for Modern Families

BIFF RAVEN-HILL

The
History
Press

WARTIME HOUSEWIFE
OLD VALUES IN A MODERN WORLD

NORTH EAST LINCOLNSHIRE COUNCIL	
01036036	
Bertrams	26/09/2013
648	£9.99

First published 2013

The History Press
The Mill, Brimscombe Port
Stroud, Gloucestershire, GL5 2QG
www.thehistorypress.co.uk

British Library Cataloguing in Publication Data.
A catalogue record for this book is available from the British Library.

ISBN 978 0 7524 9109 7
Typesetting and origination by The History Press
Printed in Great Britain

CONTENTS

CONTENTS

ACKNOWLEDGEMENTS

I would like to thank the following people for all their help, friendship and support:

George Ashley, Wilfred Ashley, Christine Beckwith, Jo Blackwell, Sophie Bradshaw, Anna Bramhall, Jennie Browning, Robert Browning, Heather Coombs, Louise Drennan, Fougasse, my grandmother Eleanor Haslingden, Marjorie James, Pam Jessiman, Paul Jessiman, Karen Lipman, Joyce Raven-Hill, Jean Skinner, Lindsey Smith, Michael Stanley, John Stothert, the people of World War II who are my inspiration, and all the readers of The Wartime Housewife website who are relentlessly interesting and entertaining.

INTRODUCTION

Dear Readers,

The Wartime Housewife has been a successful website for several years now, offering information and advice about all aspects of home and family life.

The wartime housewife is a state of mind rather than a physical entity. She sprung into being after a concerted campaign of mickey-taking by the father of my children who said that my frugal behaviour and scavenging mentality was like living with a wartime housewife.

This appealed to me very much and before long, he had designed a wonderful logo and label which I applied to food presents and the cakes and puddings with which I supplied a local café.

In 2009, by which time I was a single parent, my friend suggested that I start blogging as a foundation for future writing work. 'But I wouldn't know where to start!' I protested feebly. 'Leave it to me,' he said in a manly way and by the time I had finished cooking dinner he had set up my blog site. I began writing the next day.

The Wartime Housewife is a place where you will find old-fashioned skills and values applied to our modern lives. Life can be hard and, in this necessary period of austerity, money is tight and wastefulness is not an option. Even if money was not tight, wastefulness is wicked. Our resources are not finite and before we even think about buying new things, we should think seriously about whether we can repair or re-use the old ones.

Ask yourself: if the power goes down, will I be able to cope? Would I be prepared if there was a powercut, if a wicked fairy took away all the ready meals, if the clothing factories in Asia closed down and I had to pay more than a fiver for an outfit and couldn't get any more?

Learning to be resourceful is fun. Seeing something that you have made yourself from scratch is deeply rewarding. Scavenging in skips can reveal all sorts of treasures so start to be a 'snapper up of unconsidered trifles' and give old things new life; make the most of what you have. This is the Way of the Wartime Housewife!

But home life is so much more than being able to knit a vest out of leftover spaghetti or using old socks to make sleeping bags for hamsters. There have to be extra dimensions: fun, creativity, beauty and the development of enquiring minds, including your own. There is so much more to running a house than keeping everything pristine. One of my favourite phrases is that no one will ever write on your tombstone: 'S/he really kept up with the ironing!' But they might well write that you were a loving and trusted parent who gave guidance and security to the family.

No one will steal your dishes if you decide not to wash up in order to spend some time reading to your child. The carpets will not disappear if you occasionally choose to take your elderly parent out to lunch instead of doing the hoovering. How many times have we seen children having more fun with the box than the gift? Periodically ban the use of all things electronic, including the television; then make sure you have a bag of boxes and bits and pieces so that children can use their imagination and make something amazing. Do it with them – you'll be amazed what you can create out of the stuff that usually goes to landfill. Go outside, breathe deeply, look up and really see what's around you. Go to the library, choose a book at random and see what it has to tell you. Ask yourself, 'What can I do?' and then start to do a bit of it. I would also advise you, despite a significant amount of cleaning tips in this book, not to be too clean. We need bacteria – it is germs that exercise our immune systems and make us stronger. I'm not suggesting that we return to the glory days of running sores and consumption, but if we are not exposed to a bit of dirt our bodies will never learn to fight the dirt.

A dirty child is a happy child. Get them used to being muddy and falling out of trees from an early age. Teach them the skills to be independent so that you can send them out with confidence to play in the street, to walk in the countryside. Teach them to look closely at things, to appreciate the detail. If children get plenty of fresh air and exercise they will also develop good appetites and are less likely to obsess about what's on their plate if they're starving hungry. In my book, a fussy child goes hungry until they make the decision to eat what's put in front of them and appreciate the work and love that has gone into preparing that precious food.

Another thing I hate is when people ask if you work or if you stay at home. Anyone who has ever stayed at home will know that it is incredibly hard work running a household. I often think that parents should be recruited into high-level management jobs when their children have grown up because they have to have such a vast array of skills: husband, wife, parent, social secretary, ordnance and logistics expert, psychologist, finance expert, taxi driver, liaison officer, caterer, nurse, negotiator, leader of the United Nations … and that's just the basics.

But it's not for everyone and, if we should have learned anything over the past fifty or sixty years, it is that we have the freedom to make choices which suit our personalities and lifestyles. It's no one else's business how we conduct our home lives and the only thing that matters is that we are doing our best and no one gets neglected – including ourselves.

Everything is about balance; food, money, exercise, friendships, love – even chocolate. Yes, even chocolate. Try to find a little time in your day to do 'thinking'; not obsessing, panicking, agonising or fretting, but quiet time to reflect on who you are and what you're doing. Now stop reading this introduction and make yourself a nice hot cup of tea (an accompanying custard cream is entirely your own affair). Open the book at random and choose something to do. You won't regret it.

With love and best wishes,

Wartime Housewife

ETIQUETTE AND
MODERN MANNERS

Many people think that having an accepted code of manners and particularly etiquette is old fashioned and out-moded. Who does anyone think they are telling someone how to behave or how to hold their knife and fork? Well, let me put you straight once and for all.

Manners are there to facilitate the comfort of others. Exhibiting good manners says to a person, whether a stranger or an intimate, I care about you. You are sufficiently important to me that I recognise your needs. Manners make people comfortable and oil the wheels of social machinery. Without manners, we are barbarians.

Etiquette is there to facilitate the comfort of you. There are few things more disconcerting than being in a situation where you have no idea what to do, how to behave or what is expected of you. Etiquette gives you a safe framework for behaviour in much the same way as discipline provides a safe framework for children. If you know how to behave, others will take you more seriously. That is a fact.

Imagine that you want to write a letter to the Prime Minister complaining about the state of the nation or a particular situation that you find unacceptable. Should you start the letter: 'Oi! Cameron! What you going to do about housing, eh? It's alright for you living in a palace while I slum it in a council house etc. etc. Up yours, Joe Bloggs,' there is a reasonable chance that you won't get a helpful response.

If, however, you start the letter correctly, taking into account the nature of your audience, such as: 'Dear Prime Minister, I wish to draw to your attention the problems that people in my area are experiencing with regard to housing etc. etc. Yours sincerely, Joe Bloggs,' you are far more likely to get a sensible and considered reply.

And this is really the bottom line. Manners and etiquette are there so that you have the ability to blend into any situation by assessing the nature of the people you're with. I hold my knife and fork exactly the same if I'm sitting in front of the telly with a microwaved spag bol on a tray, as I would if I were dining with the Duke of Poshington. However, my manners and behaviour might just become less formal if I was out on the lash with Irish Alice. Much, much less formal …

TABLE MANNERS

General Manners for the Family

Sharing food is one of the most pleasant and companiable things people can do. Enjoying a meal carefully prepared for

A rather lovely family group, having a rather lovely family meal. From *Housewife Magazine*; November 1943

you is a lovely thing and taking the trouble to cook good food is another way of saying, 'I care about you,' which is the essence of manners.

Nowadays the ritual of eating is much more relaxed than it ever has been, but if the ground rules become second nature, it is one less thing to have to think about.

Cutlery

Forks on the left, knives and spoons on the right and the guest should work from the outside inwards, course by course.

If a fork is used without a knife, it is held in the right hand with the tines (prongs) pointing up. Always hold it as near to the end of the handle as you can. The fork should rest on the middle finger which is supported by the outer two fingers.

Eating with just a fork

If a knife and fork are being used together, the fork should be held like a knife with the tines pointing downward. It is acceptable nowadays to turn the fork over momentarily in order to scoop up food that has been pushed onto it by the knife. In that case the food should be pushed onto the inner side of the fork, otherwise you might poke your companion on the left with your elbow.

Eating persistently with the tines of the fork turned upward is not acceptable. The knife should be held as in the illustration and never held like a pen.

If you are eating with a spoon alone, it should be held in the right hand, just like a solo fork. If a fork and spoon are used together, the fork should be used in the left hand with the tines pointing downward. The spoon is the receptacle in this case and the fork as the guide.

Soup should be sipped from the side of the spoon unless it is a really thick, chunky pottage which would be impossible. The spoon should be dipped sideways into the soup and pushed away from you so that any drips fall back into the bowl. When the bowl is nearly empty, tip it away from you slightly to get the last bit out of the bowl.

Pausing and finishing eating: It is correct to lay your cutlery down after each mouthful while you chew and swallow. To indicate with your cutlery that you are merely pausing, the knife and fork (or fork and spoon) should be laid neatly in the twenty past eight position of the clock with the tines of the fork pointing down.

Eating with a knife and fork

Eating with a fork and spoon

Eating soup

When you have finished, lay the knife and fork (or fork and spoon) neatly side by side, in the six-thirty or twenty-five past five position, with the tines of the fork pointing upward. This indicates to both guests and waiting staff that you have finished.

How to place your knife and fork when you pause from eating

How to place your knife and fork when you have finished eating

Food, guests and seconds: If you have guests at the family table and that guest wants a second helping, the family should always hold back and offer the food to the guest. A muttered warning of 'FHB' (family hold back) to an over-enthusiastic child can dissipate any awkwardness.

General Behaviour

Everyone should come to the table when called or at the time appointed by the cook.

You should go to the loo and wash your hands before sitting down to eat, but if you must leave, discreetly ask to be excused and return to the table as quickly as possible.

Conversation is extremely good for slowing down the speed at which you eat, and it is proven that eating slowly is much better for your digestion and if you're trying to lose weight. Use the meal table as an opportunity to catch up on the day and show interest in what other people are doing.

Never talk with your mouth full. You should only ever put as much food on your fork as can be chewed and swallowed quickly if you need to speak.

Be attentive to the needs of the others at the table. Pass drinks down if someone's glass is empty and always offer drinks, food or gravy to other people before using it yourself.

When you have finished eating, do not get up and leave the table before everyone else has finished. Remember to say thank you to the cook for your food.

The people who have not cooked should clear the table and wash up or load the dishwasher.

These behaviours should be the same whether you are sitting at a table or sitting on the sofa with a tray.

ENTERTAINING

Entertaining is much more fun if you get out all your best china and glasses and put on a bit of a show. Ordinary life is too dull not to make the effort from time to time.

The first thing to remember is that when you issue an invitation, make sure that you are absolutely clear about what sort of event you are hosting and what is expected of your guests so there is no confusion. It would be desperately embarrassing for your guests to turn up to an informal affair wearing full evening dress and with their valet in tow. OK, so I'm exaggerating about the valet, but you get my drift. See the section on 'Correspondence' for help with composing invitations.

Cutlery

When laying place settings, the tines of the forks should always point upwards and the blade of the knife should always face inwards towards the plate. Forks go on the left and knives and

From left to right: fork for starter, fork for main course, fish fork, pudding fork, knife for main course, knife for starter or butter, fish knife, pudding spoon, soup spoon, tea or coffee spoon

An informal place setting for soup, main course and pudding with wine. What do you mean you don't do this every evening?

Place setting for soup, main course and pudding with sherry, red wine and champagne – formal

Place setting for starter, main course and pudding with water, red wine, white wine and port

spoons on the right. You should start using the cutlery on the outside first and gradually work inwards.

Crockery and Glasses

Seating

I am always inclined to have a seating plan so that you can think in advance who will get on with whom and which guest should be kept as far away as possible from another.

From left to right: dinner plate, side plate, soup bowl

From left to right: water tumbler, red wine, white wine, champagne, sherry or port

Place setting for soup, main course and pudding with sherry, red wine and champagne – formal with mitred napkin

Place cards – these should be handwritten and nicely presented. For informal dinners just the first name is acceptable. For formal events, the full name including courtesy title should be used, e.g. Mr Joseph Bloggs, His Royal Highness the Duke of Poshington, Dr Josephine Bloggs, The Rev. Josephine Bloggs etc. Technically a wife should be referred to as Mrs Joe

Bloggs but I think I would flounce out of a party in a huff if anyone addressed me thus. It is the twenty-first century after all.

Wines

If you are at all unsure as to which wines to serve with which course, the following rule of thumb is pretty safe.

SOUP – sherry
SHELLFISH AND FISH – dry white wine
WHITE MEAT OR POULTRY – a dry white wine is always safe or you may prefer a very light red or a rosé
RED MEAT AND GAME – red wine, something full-bodied like a Burgundy or for less robust flavours, something lighter such as a Bordeaux
CHEESE – you can carry on with the red wine if you like but it would seem a shame not to get a decent port out at this point
PUDDINGS OR DESSERTS – a lovely sweet wine such as a Sauterne or a Muscatel is a lovely treat

Serving Wine

OPENING – red wine should be uncorked and allowed to stand for a while to achieve room temperature. This is called *chambré*-ing (pronounced 'Shom-bray'). An old red needs only an hour whereas a new red needs to chambré for several hours.
DECANTING – ideally vintage port and red wines should be decanted slowly into the decanter through a strainer to remove the sediment. White wines and champagne are served straight from the bottle.
PORT – port is brought to the table at the same time as the cheese and/or dessert. The host should serve the person on his/her right, pour himself some and then pass the decanter to the left. Port is always passed clockwise and each guest should help himself. It is up to the guests to make sure the decanter keeps moving and that everyone has an elegant sufficiency.

Napkins

Firstly, they are called napkins not serviettes.

If you are having a formal dinner then napkins should be linen and large. Paper napkins are fine for informal dinners and can be more easily co-ordinated with your colour scheme.

If you like to fold napkins into interesting shapes, then they should be placed in the middle of the place setting. If they are simply folded, then they should be laid neatly on the side plate.

As soon as you sit down at the table, you should unfold your napkin and lay it neatly across your lap. Do not tuck it into your shirt front, gentlemen, please. There's no need to slobber on your napkin, just use it to dab your mouth or discreetly wipe your fingers.

When the meal is finished and you leave the table, do not fold your napkin; just put it back on the table.

Food

When choosing your menu, spare a thought for your guests and whether certain foods will be awkward or messy to eat. This doesn't matter so much for informal parties, but if your guests have turned up in silk frocks and expensive waistcoats, they won't want to risk dripping butter or spaghetti down their fronts.

And on the subject of food, may I just point out that 'dessert' means fruit or nuts and pudding is everything else. 'Sweets' are humbugs or fruit pastilles.

Special Diets or Allergies

It is incumbent upon your guests to notify you if they have special dietary requirements. If they turn up and can't eat anything it is their own fault. It is extremely impolite to refuse food without very good reason. If you really can't eat something, take a tiny portion and leave it on the side of your plate. Equally, the host should refrain from drawing attention to you in this situation.

I was once at a dinner party and was served *foie gras*, which I will not eat under any circumstances. I took a tiny piece and left it on the side of my plate. My host noticed and asked loudly why I wasn't eating it and I was forced to explain my ethical objections, which was rude to the host and uncomfortable for the other guests. Manners are all about comfort – physical and emotional.

Dinner Parties without Staff

Now, I'm not suggesting that we all maintain a full staff chez nous, but obviously dinner in a restaurant where one is being served by waiters requires different manners to a party in one's home.

By far the best method of serving food at a dinner party is for the meat to be served by the host and the plates then passed down the table to the guests. The guests then serve themselves with vegetables and condiments. This is convenient, friendly and doesn't take the host away from the table.

If you are holding a serving dish for another diner to help herself, offer the dish to the person on your left who will then serve herself, replace the serving implements side by side in the dish, take the dish and then offer it to the person on her left. Thank the person serving but do not attempt to continue a conversation while the food is being passed round.

Do offer to help your host but never bang on about it. It is the guests' responsibility to be charming and agreeable and the host has probably worked out a way of doing things which will cause the least disruption and your insistence on helping may end up being a hindrance.

Conduct

As I said in the last paragraph, a guest is required to be pleasant and charming and to extend conversation to people on either side of him not just one person. A guest should mingle and stimulate conversation.

If the person next to you is unutterably dull or uncommunicative, try to draw him out with questions about his work or hobbies. Conversation should flow both ways but some people are just ignorant. If you cannot escape, draw in another diner from across the table and share the pain. If you are at an after dinner party, draw the person out for as long as you can but then make your excuses and leave, possibly because you've been hailed by someone on the other side of the room.

TIMING – never be late, but absolutely never be early. Hang around in the car round the corner rather than turn up half an hour early and throw your host into a panic.

INTRODUCTIONS – a host should keep an eye on the guests at all times and make it her business to introduce people. However, sometimes a host can have a cerebral power cut and if it's obvious that they've forgotten your name, step forward politely, smile and tell the other person your name to save your host embarrassment.

LEAVING THE TABLE – when dinner is finished, the hostess may ask you all to go to another room with more comfortable chairs. However, modern houses are sometimes too small to accommodate everyone in the sitting room and it may be more convivial to remain at the table. Wait for a signal from the host that the formal part of the evening is over.

LADIES WITHDRAW – in times past, the women would withdraw and the men would stay at the table for port and cigars. This may seem like a sexist thing to do, but in a large and more formal gathering it makes perfect sense. The women may want to go to the loo, touch up their make-up, hoik their tights up and have a giggle with the other women, which may be less easy in mixed company where one is obliged to mix equally with both sexes. However, this separation should not carry on for more than twenty minutes or half an hour before gathering together again.

Smoking

It is excessively bad manners to smoke at the table unless the host takes the lead and lights up or offers cigarettes round. It is far better to wait until the end of the meal and nip outside for a fag if you need one.

Nowadays, when smoking has effectively been criminalised without the inconvenience of the government relinquishing their revenue from it, it is possible to go to a party where no one smokes at all.

It is interesting to note in the 1981 *Debrett's* that they suggest that cigarettes should be made available to guests and placed in suitable boxes or containers and that ash trays should be large and plentiful with a layer of sand in the bottom to prevent smouldering and odour.

Difficulties

Most of the time, a host must simply grin and bear it if a guest is misbehaving in a fairly minor way or being a complete bore. Quite honestly, it's often better to simply not invite someone who you know cannot be trusted to behave or who gets drunk and obnoxious. Don't be afraid to enlist the help of another guest if things are getting out of hand.

CONVERSATION – as the host, only you can judge whether a conversation is fun and stimulating or uncomfortable or inappropriate. It is wise to choose your guests according to the sort of conversations you know to expect from them. Mixing a socialist worker with a fully paid-up blackshirt might be amusing, but make sure you have a comprehensive first aid kit to hand.

OBNOXIOUS GUESTS – if a guest pursues a conversation which is upsetting or annoying someone, the host should try to steer the conversation in another direction or, if possible, move them away and introduce them to someone else. If a guest is known to bang on about a particular topic it might be worth having a quiet word before they arrive and ask them to be sensitive to the interests of the other guests.

Likewise, if someone constantly repeats a particular story, you might tactfully say (with a mischievous look), 'I've always loved that story, ever since you told it to me ten years ago!'

SOCIAL BLUNDERS – don't make a fuss. If someone inadvertently makes an appalling blunder such as, 'Bloody hell, isn't Clive an unspeakable bore!', and Clive happens to be your husband, immediately make the person aware of this fact and try to mitigate the offence by saying something like, 'I know Clive can be rather forceful/shy/single-minded, but he's very passionate/diffident/ enthusiastic about what he does,' or, 'Oh most people find him rather entertaining.' Sometimes, however, it's best to shut up or turn the gaffe into a joke.

TROUBLESOME BEHAVIOUR – getting drunk, stoned or obnoxious is not acceptable. If someone gets completely out of hand, get another guest to help you remove them or put them in a cab and send them home. I once locked my host in a spare room at a dinner party until he had sobered up; no one should have to deal with that.

DRUGS – are illegal and the presence of them at a party may make some of your guests uncomfortable or even compromise them if they hold public positions. Again, it is up to the host to make the position clear on this at the start.

ACCIDENTS – with the best will in the world accidents happen. If you break or spill something, discreetly ask for your host's help in clearing up. As a host, you should be prepared for such an eventuality and make as little fuss as possible. If something is spilled on clothing, quietly withdraw and sponge yourself down. If it's a massive spillage, the host may offer to lend you an alternative garment.

SOCIAL BEHAVIOUR

Introductions

It is very important to introduce people you meet to your companions, whether at a social event or bumping into them in the street. Nothing complicated, 'Oh hello Betty! Do you know James?' or, 'Mrs Bloggs – Mr Rumpole'.

If, like me, you have difficulty even remembering the names of your children, the safest thing to do is say, "Of course, you two know each other?" and, if this is not the case, the friends should then help you out by smiling and saying, "I'm Ada Benyon," and the other person should say, "Barnaby Rudge". Problem solved.

If, however, you have no intention of introducing someone – for whatever reason – that person should discreetly walk away and save everyone embarrassment. You can grill them about it later.

Conversations

How many times have you met someone, either formally or casually, who makes no attempt at conversation whatsoever? This is bad manners in itself, as it is the responsibility of guests to mix and converse pleasantly with the others.

Personally, I have an extreme hatred of being asked, "So, what do you do?" and I have to be careful not to answer rudely, "When?" We are not defined by what we do for a living and, although this may be interesting, it is just as interesting to talk about one's interests. It is possibly best to start with non-controversial or current subjects.

Opening conversations might be:

- What are you reading at the moment?
- If you could travel to only one place in the world, where would it be?
- Have you been watching the tennis/rugby/football?
- Do you know many people here?
- What lovely wine! Are you much of a connoisseur?
- I went to such and such a film/play/concert the other night. Have you seen it?
- Did you see/have you been following such and such on the TV? Wasn't it brilliant?

Eating Out

If you're putting together a group to go out to eat it is important that your friends know what sort of place you're going to so that they can dress appropriately and know whether they can afford it or not. Try to be aware of your friends' financial situations and don't embarrass them by going to somewhere horribly expensive if they are on a low income. Unless you're paying, of course, in which case you should make that clear.

If you're going on a date, I would always recommend going Dutch initially so that no one is compromised. There is no reason why a man should automatically pay for a woman and, once again, the arrangement should be made clear so that no one is under any illusions. Or, if someone pays on one occasion, suggest or even insist that the other pays next time.

This applies also to any social outing whether it's the cinema, bowling, dancing, or a concert.

General Manners

Yet again we're back to manners being a way of accommodating other people and showing that you care about their welfare, whether it's a stranger or your partner. Some behaviours are outmoded and unnecessary whereas others are appropriate in a formal situation or with older people who have different expectations.

Feminism went through a phase where some women were offended if a man offered her his seat on the bus or attempted to carry her shopping. Women are no longer the weaker sex and they, mostly, have equality on every level including income.

I am an equalist. I believe that good manners should be extended to everyone round us, whether male or female, young or old, and courtesies apply where appropriate rather than as an historical continuum.

Therefore:

SEATS – always offer your seat to someone who needs it more than you – male or female, particularly if they are elderly, infirm or pregnant.

DOORS – hold doors open for people and smile as you do so. If someone holds a door for you, smile and say thank you.

BURDENS – if you see someone struggling, offer to help them. If they don't want your help they can say so.

CARRYING SHOPPING – always offer to carry, or at least share, the shopping of someone you're with, male or female, especially if they are older than you.

REFUSING A COURTESY – if you really don't want help always be courteous in your refusal; a straightforward "No, thank you very much, I'm fine" is perfectly acceptable, whereas saying "You chauvinist pig – I'm perfectly capable. You sicken me!" is rude in the extreme and generally considered unhelpful.

VISITING – never drop in on anyone unannounced unless you know for sure that it is ok within the bounds of your friendship. We all have mobile phones now, so just make a quick call to allow your friend time to tidy up, put some clothes on, shove their lover in the wardrobe or to tell you that your visit is not convenient.

We are all incredibly busy these days and the afternoon that you call might be the only few hours that person has to do a particular job, to rest or have a bath. If this is the case, it's perfectly acceptable to tell the person that you're busy but suggest another time when it would be convenient for you both. The meeting will be a happier one.

MOBILE PHONES – mobiles are both a blessing and a curse but, like everything else, they must be used courteously. I hope it goes without saying that they should be turned off during concerts, films etc., but I would suggest that they should also be switched off at any social event, unless it needs to be kept on for a babysitter or sick relative. In this case, apologise in advance to your friends and explain why it's necessary.

If you are with someone, you should give them your full attention, not be constantly breaking off to read Twitter or look at amusing pictures of cats with poor grammar and a craving for cheeseburgers.

ADAPTING BEHAVIOUR – always be aware of your audience; an older person usually expects more courtesy and deference than your peers and you should be extra attentive to variations in company. This includes swearing and slang.

HELPING STRANGERS – I always address strangers in a formal way so as not to appear threatening and, if the person is elderly, I always refer to them as 'Sir' or 'Ma'am'. Asking, "Are you alright, Sir?" reassures them that you are showing respect and are possibly less likely to steal their pension book.

IN THE WORKPLACE – if a new person arrives in your place of work, go out of your way to show them the ropes and introduce them round the office, if no one else has done so. Refrain from gossip or malice about existing colleagues as it is up to the new person to draw their own conclusions. Show them the loos, the coffee room and the photocopier, and fill them in on social protocol and habits. Reassure them that no question is stupid and that it's better to ask than get something wrong.

GUESTS IN YOUR HOME – go out of your way to make them feel comfortable and at ease in your home. Again, show them where everything is and let them know if there are any rules about shoes, security etc. If they are staying over, make sure that their room is clean and comfortable, put out fresh towels on the bed and make sure they have everything they need.

A NOTE ABOUT SHOES – it is incredibly bad manners to ask someone to remove their shoes when they enter your house unless it is on cultural or religious grounds. It is embarrassing and inconvenient for your guests and implies that they are dirty. If you're that worried about your cream carpets then maybe you have chosen unwisely.

Obviously, if someone comes yomping in off the moors with mud-caked walking boots or heavily manured wellies, no one will be offended if you ask them to remove their footwear at the door, or pop down some newspaper for them to do so. Natural good manners will inform you how to deal with this situation sensitively and a courteous guest will never inconvenience you with cacky boots.

CORRESPONDENCE

I rarely get any letters through my door that aren't junk mail or demands for money and it's such a joy to find a handwritten envelope with an interesting or exotic stamp on it from a friend or relative. Although emails and texts are hugely convenient for so many things, they do not take the place of invitations, thank you letters or birthday cards.

When you do write a letter, it is important to know how to structure it correctly and how to address an envelope.

Addressing an Envelope

With so many letters being mail-merged, or put in window envelopes, it is easy to forget that there is a correct way to write an envelope. There is also a courtesy involved in writing clearly so that the poor postman stands a chance of reading it correctly and the letter getting to the right place.

The correct way to address a handwritten envelope

Start the address half way down the envelope and a third of the way across. The address should be staggered, with a comma at the end of each line and the postcode on a separate line at the end or, if space is short, next to the county with a full stop after it.

It is usual to write either 'Mrs J Bloggs' for a more formal letter, or 'Jo Bloggs' for a less formal letter.

The stamp goes in the top right hand corner about ½cm from the edge.

It is sensible to put the sender's address on the back and many people have little printed stickers made, which are extremely useful.

Thank You Letters

People seem to be sending fewer and fewer thank you letters. I recognise that we live in less formal times, and I wouldn't expect a thank you letter from someone who had opened a gift in front of me, although my friend, Lady Marjorie, insists on writing thank you letters to everyone for gifts or hospitality and I find it a rather pleasing habit.

As a child, I became very lax about sending thank you letters and eventually godmothers and aunts simply stopped sending gifts and I don't blame them. It is essential to get children into the habit of writing letters so that it becomes second nature as they progress into adulthood. Start with gifts to their friends for birthday parties and make them write it themselves or at least write the 'Dear …', the detail of the present and their names. I get very annoyed if thank you letters are not forthcoming from children after a party.

I always keep a stock of cards in, both for emergency birthdays and for thank you letters. I have a small lidded box in my office, clearly marked 'Cards' which also contains a book of first class stamps. It's important to write your thank you letters as soon after the event as possible; sending it a couple of weeks later smacks of guilt and tardiness.

A thank you letter doesn't have to be a great long epistle, but, in the same way that giving a gift or extending hospitality tells people you care about them, a thank you letter says that you have appreciated the thing enough to take the time to write a letter. However, the letter should say slightly more than simply 'Thanks for my present. Love Clarence'.

I would suggest including the following elements:

THANKING FOR A GIFT — start with an appropriate greeting: 'Hi Yoda!' to your Granny may not be appropriate. 'Dear So and so' is normally best.

Thank them specifically for the gift and congratulate them on their choice: 'Thank you so much for the lovely earrings; they are just the right style and I couldn't have chosen better myself.'

Suggest how you might use the gift: 'I have a dress with which the earrings will go beautifully.'

Add a little bit of chat about the event: 'I had a lovely birthday and I did such and such …'

Finish by thanking them again and adding your sign off, such as, 'Lots of love,' or 'With best wishes' etc.

THANKING FOR HOSPITALITY — thank them for being invited to the specific event: 'Thank you so much for inviting me to your dinner party on Saturday.'

Comment positively on the food, the skill of the cook and the delightfulness of the other guests. 'The meal was so well thought out and the fricasseed koala was a particular triumph. It was lovely to meet so and so again and wasn't so and so fascinating — her knowledge of pole dancing for the disabled was quite extraordinary!'

However, as we know, there are times when a gift or an event has been absolutely unspeakable; the gift is practically insulting or the food was damned near poisonous. There are lots of words and phrases that can be employed which are totally ambiguous and meaningless but still sound as though you are paying a compliment:

'Well, that was really something'
'What an unusual/imaginative gift/dish'
'How clever of you to think of that'
'What an unexpected gift'
'How generous of you to think of me'
'You really are an extraordinary cook'
'I would never have thought of that for myself and it's so nice to be introduced to new things'
'You always come up with such interesting gifts/menu ideas'

But even a one-liner is better than nothing and an email or text is not ideal but, again, is better than nothing.

Write thank you letters; allow someone the pleasure of a letter that is praising them, not demanding money. Be gracious and charming and eventually it will be visited upon you tenfold.

Invitations

If you are holding a small party or dinner party, it's a sensible precaution to invite your friends over the telephone to make sure they can come and then send a written invitation out with details of time, place, and the type of event.

INFORMAL INVITATIONS – nowadays, many people can produce invitations in lots of jolly and imaginative ways on their computers, but the contents should be the same as it always has been. The host should make it very clear to the invitees what kind of event it is, where it is, what time they should arrive and leave, and what the dress code is.

FORMAL INVITATIONS – a formal invitation should be printed on good quality card and can either be printed in its entirety with the name of the invitee hand written neatly in the top left-hand corner or merely a printed card saying:

▼

▼

Mrs J Bloggs
at Home

42 Acacia Avenue,
Long Snoddington,
Northumberland,
NB73 4LX.
Tel: 01752 988111

The details of the event should be handwritten underneath and the invitee's name handwritten in the top left-hand corner. RSVP is not needed if the person has already accepted over the phone or in person, but you may wish to put 'To Remind' or 'PM' (*Pour Memoire*) above the address.

ANSWERING AN INVITATION – always answer as soon as you can to make things easier for your host. If the invitation is addressed to 'Josephine' reply in a friendly way: 'Dear Oliver,'. If the invitation is addressed to 'Mrs Bloggs' reply more formally: 'Dear Mr Twist,'.

DISPLAYING INVITATIONS – it is slightly bad form to display invitations in a prominent place where visitors will see them. If you have lots it might be seen as boasting and could create unrest if someone sees an invitation to an event to which they have not been invited. Far better to put them in a pile or on a noticeboard by your desk or in a private room for you to deal with on your own.

General Letter Writing

There are too many forms of address for me to go into in a book of this size but, once again, assessing your recipient will guide you as to the correct form of writing. If you find yourself constantly corresponding with royalty, bishops or high court judges, I strongly recommend that you buy a recent copy of *Debrett's*. This invaluable book will tell you everything you need to know in order not to disgrace yourself in front of the Earl of Poshington.

Your letter should always have your address at the top in the centre or for less formal, handwritten letters at the top right of the paper. The date should appear either underneath the address or at the left just above the address of the recipient. Dear So and So should then appear several lines underneath the recipient's address.

PERSONAL BUT FORMAL LETTERS – should begin, 'Dear Mrs Bloggs,' and end, 'Yours sincerely'.
PERSONAL BUT INFORMAL LETTERS – should begin, 'Dear or My Dear Josephine,' and end, 'With best wishes,' 'Yours affectionately,' 'With love,' or, 'Lots of love,' depending on your intimacy with the recipient.
BUSINESS LETTERS – should begin, 'Dear Sir or Madam,' and end, 'Yours faithfully'.

CHILDREN

Children will only exhibit good manners if they are taught good manners at home and these are reinforced at school. Just as discipline gives them boundaries that make them feel safe and loved, so manners help them to feel at ease in any environment and will make them much more pleasant people to be with.

I absolutely do not approve of the sentiment that 'children should be seen and not heard'. They should absolutely be allowed to join adult conversations where appropriate because otherwise how will they learn how to conduct adult conversations? This also allows them to realise that there is a wider world being discussed and that they are not the centre of the universe.

I could rant on for several large leather-bound volumes about bringing up children but I will spare you that and simply address the business of manners and behaviour, and leave the rest for another time.

This little girl even holds her spoon properly for her teddies

Mealtimes

Children should sit at the table, hold their cutlery properly (see the chapter on Table Manners) and display the same manners as the grown-ups.

They should come to meals promptly. I have an old school bell that I ring to save me shouting all over the house and they seem to respond to this well.

They should be encouraged to go to the loo and wash their hands before meals, but if they need to leave the table, they should ask, 'Please may I be excused?' and then return promptly to the table.

When the meal is finished they should say thank you and ask to get down.

I know a lot of families feed the children early and the adults eat later, but personally I prefer to eat together as a family so that they learn adult manners and the etiquette of conversation as early as possible. This way, if you take them to a restaurant, good behaviour will be second nature.

Children should eat what is put in front of them and clear their plates. It is up to the adult to serve appropriate portions and it is far better to give a child a smaller amount and give them the option of 'seconds' if they're still hungry.

Fussiness is extremely bad manners and must be stamped upon as early as possible. Fussy adults are a massive pain in the arse, so nip it in the bud when they're children.

Children of 'all classes' enjoying a free meal at an early state primary school in Wales

Mealtime conversation should be appropriate to the whole family but children must be taught not to shout and not to interrupt when an adult or sibling is talking. Adults should extend the same courtesy to the children and lead by example.

If children behave badly, fight or whinge at the table, a first warning should be given to stop. If they continue, they should be sent to their rooms and the meal forfeited. This may seem harsh but the behaviour will soon stop and no child will deliberately starve themselves to death.

Conversation

Children should be encouraged to talk to people and learn that listening is as important as speaking. Again, teach by example.

Never ridicule a child or make them look stupid in public or private, as this will discourage them from participating in conversations and probably make them rude and sullen.

Children should always address adults as Mr or Mrs, unless they have been told otherwise. Nowadays, most family friends are happy to be called by their first names, but children should not assume.

They should never interrupt an adult conversation unless it is absolutely urgent. 'Blood or flames' is what I tell the boys. A courteous adult will listen and include a child where appropriate.

If a child is being annoying at a social gathering, the parent should issue a quiet reprimand and tell them to pipe down or leave.

Behaviour Outside

Although it's not fair to inflict impossibly boring situations on children as a regular exercise, they do have to learn that there are times when they must simply grin and bear boring events without making a fuss.

GOING TO CHURCH – is such an event. Even if you're not a churchgoer, everyone will end up in one at some time, for weddings and funerals if nothing else. As usual, I could talk at length about the influence of the Bible on art, literature, music, architecture and many other aspects of British culture and it's hard to have a proper understanding of these things without some basic knowledge. We all have to behave properly in church and it is worthwhile taking them to a place of worship from time to time, not only as a cultural experience but also as an exercise in practising restrained behaviour.

PUBS – I'm a big believer in socialising children as soon as they know how to behave but there must be some places where adults can go without children running about the place. The pub is one such place and I don't think that children should be in pubs after about 8 p.m. unless there is no alternative, and they are very quiet and don't disturb anyone. No one should have to moderate their language in an adult environment because a child has invaded the joint.

RESTAURANTS – children should not be taken into public eating places until you are confident that their manners and behaviour are up to it. If table manners are drummed into them at home, they will behave well automatically in a restaurant or café and that will make your social life so much easier. They should never, ever be allowed to run around, shout or interrupt other diners. This should apply in McDonald's or La Gavroche.

PARTIES – if it is appropriate for your children to be at a party, e.g. if it is during the day or early evening, explain to them that they have equal duties as hosts. Encourage them to offer snacks and drinks round and to unobtrusively engage the guests in polite conversation. This will make them feel important and needed and they will be less likely to misbehave.

APPROPRIATE RUNNING AROUND AND SHOUTING – I insist that all children are better behaved if they have plenty of fresh air and exercise. They must also have time alone with their peers as they get older and this is the time when they can get all the running around and shouting out of their systems, to say nothing of practising all the social skills that you've taught them already.

2

HOUSEHOLD ESSENTIALS

CONVERSION TABLE

Solid Weight Conversions		Oven Temperature Conversions		
IMPERIAL	METRIC	°F	GAS MARK	°C
½oz	15g	225	¼	110
1oz	30g	250	½	120
2oz	60g	275	1	140
3oz	90g	300	2	150
4oz (¼lb)	120g	325	3	160
5oz	150g	350	4	175
6oz	180g	375	5	190
8oz (½lb)	240g	400	6	200
12oz (¾lb)	360g	425	7	220
16oz (1lb)	480g	450	8	230
		475	9	240
		500	10	260

Liquid Conversions			
IMPERIAL	METRIC	US CUPS	Quantities in recipes are usually given in one or all three measures. Follow ONLY ONE set of measures and on no account mix them up
½floz	15ml	1tbsp (level)	
1floz	30ml	⅛ cup	
2floz	60ml	¼ cup	
3floz	90ml	⅜ cup	
4floz	125ml	½ cup	
5floz (¼pint)	150ml	⅔ cup	1 UK pint = 20floz
6floz	175ml	¾ cup	1 US pint = 16floz 1 litre = 33floz
8floz	250ml	1 cup (½pint)	(1 US quart)
10floz (½pint)	300ml	1 ¼ cups	
12floz	375ml	1 ½ cups	oz = ounce
16floz	500ml	2 cups (1 US pint)	fl = fluid g = gram
20floz (1 pint)	600ml	2 ½ cups	ml = millilitre
1 ½ pints	900ml	3 ¾ cups	qt = quart lb = pound
1 ¾ pints	1 litre	1 qt (4 cups)	tsp = teaspoon tbsp = tablespoon
2 pints (1qt)	1 ¼ litres	1 ¼ quarts	
2 ⅓ pints	1 ½ litres	3 US pints	
3 ¼ pints	2 litres	2 quarts	

Measuring Without Scales

1 gently rounded tbsp flour	= 1oz
1 level tbsp sugar	= ½oz
1 tbsp jam, golden syrup or honey	= 2oz
½ pint glass of flour	= 4–5 ounces
½ pint glass sugar	= 8oz (½lb)
A piece of butter, lard or margarine about the size of a small egg	= 2oz
7 tbsp liquid	= ¼ pint

THE BASIC STORE CUPBOARD

This may seem like a lot, but I bet if you were to rummage through your cupboards, freezer and fridge right now, you would find a lot more, of a lot less use, and several things that would arouse the ridicule of your peers. From this basic list, you can feed a family for a week, perhaps only needing to top up with milk and bread. Remember also that you can buy fresh items such as onions, peppers and leeks when they're cheap, chop them up and put them in bags in the freezer for use when you haven't got any or can't get them fresh.

Larder	
Tinned chopped tomatoes	Red lentils
Tinned kidney beans	Green lentils
Tinned sweetcorn	Rice – easy cook
Tinned tuna	Tomato purée
Tinned mackerel	Sugar – white and dark brown
Baked beans	Flour – plain white, self-raising white, plain wholemeal
Custard powder	
Cocoa	Pasta – spaghetti and something else
Raspberry jam	
Worcestershire sauce	Cooking oil – preferably olive but sunflower is perfectly good
Soy sauce	
Porridge oats	Mustard powder
Stock cubes – chicken, beef and vegetable	Lemon juice
	Honey
Tinned whole peaches	Golden syrup
Condensed milk	Raisins
Tea and coffee	
Assorted dried herbs, especially: parsley, mixed herbs, sage, thyme, oregano, bay leaves	Spices: cumin, coriander, turmeric, paprika, ginger, chilli powder

Freezer	Fridge
Whole chicken	Milk
Fish fillets – coley or bass are	Eggs
cheap and as tasty as anything	Butter
else	Bread
Fish fingers	Onions
Mince	Garlic
Lamb's liver – very cheap,	Carrots
versatile and incredibly tasty	Cheddar – nice strong stuff
Vegetables – peas, whole green	Long-life double cream (fresh is
beans, spinach, corn on the cob	always better but we're talking
Bread (a few slices can be kept	emergency backup here)
in the smallest freezer)	Bananas
Sausages	

BASIC KITCHEN EQUIPMENT

It's very tempting to fill your kitchen with unnecessary gadgets but all that happens is that one ends up with a kitchen full of stuff, half of which you never use. I am assuming that you understand your own needs regarding crockery, cutlery, mugs and glasses, a kettle and a toaster; I will, therefore, concentrate on essential everyday equipment that you need if you are planning to cook properly at least some of the time, plus a few things that would be useful when entertaining or if you regularly make certain things.

It may sound like rather basic information, but if you are only just starting to get interested in cooking, it's very easy to go over the top. A large and expensive food processor sounds like a great idea, but unless you have a sizeable kitchen where it can be out on the worktop all the time, you may find that you simply can't be bothered to get it out of the cupboard and £200 of kit will languish, sobbing to itself, in the deepest darkest cupboard, with naught but the silverfish for company, dreaming of making coleslaw for fifty people. Resist. Keep it simple.

Essential Equipment

I SET OF THREE DIFFERENT SIZED MIXING BOWLS (if you get ovenproof they are more versatile still)

I SET OF SAUCEPANS e.g. 2 large, I medium, I small

2 CASSEROLE DISHES – I large, I medium or small, suitable for oven or hob

2 FRYING PANS – I large and deep, I omelette type

I PIE DISH – medium

I LASAGNE DISH

2 HEATPROOF JUGS for gravy, custard etc.

I COLANDER

I SIEVE

2 CHOPPING BOARDS – I large, I small

SEVERAL WOODEN SPOONS

I FISH SLICE

I SOUP LADLE

I POTATO MASHER

I LARGE SPOON

I SLOTTED SPOON

I WHISK

I PASTRY BRUSH

I FLEXIBLE SCRAPER

I VEGETABLE PEELER

I ROLLING PIN

I TIN OPENER

I CORKSCREW

I MEASURING JUG

I SET OF SCALES

I STICK BLENDER – vital

I ELECTRIC MINI CHOPPER – marvelous for breadcrumbs, nuts or any smaller quantities

I ELECTRIC HAND MIXER

I LARGE BAKING SHEET

I ROASTING TIN

I 12-HOLE BUN TIN

I 7X10IN BAKING TIN

2 7IN CAKE TINS – preferably loose bottomed

I COOLING RACK

I SET OF PASTRY CUTTERS

I GRATER which does coarse, fine, slices etc.

I LEMON SQUEEZER

KNIVES – it is better to have I large and I small really good quality, sharp knives than loads of thin, bendy blunt ones (with which you are more likely to injure yourself)

I SET OF TUPPERWARES – assorted sizes including a large one for cakes etc.

SEVERAL ODD SAUCERS – as spoon rests, for pre-weighed ingredients, to put mugs on; they are very useful

LARGE SHARP KITCHEN SCISSORS

I RADIO – more entertaining and less distracting than a television

FREEZERPROOF CONTAINERS – washed out takeaway boxes are perfect for this

Additional useful items

I **SLOW COOKER** – very useful if you're out at work

I **ICE CREAM MAKER** – you can make ice cream out of almost anything

I **CAFETIERE**

STORAGE JARS – not necessary but make it much easier to see what you've got, especially if you label them clearly, which you would need to for flour

I **LARGE FLAN DISH**

2 **ILB LOAF TINS**

I **GARLIC CRUSHER**

I **FLOUR/SUGAR SHAKER**

I **KITCHEN BLOW TORCH** – for quick browning and sugar melting

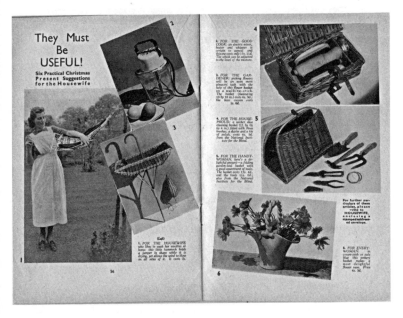

Article from *Housewife Magazine*; 1939

BASIC CLEANING EQUIPMENT

You really don't need to go over the top with this. Companies will try to seduce you into buying all sorts of things but don't fall for it until you've demonstrated the need through time, money or utility.

1 **VACUUM CLEANER** – get the best you can afford. If your carpets are clean the whole room looks clean

1 **STURDY MOP AND BUCKET**

A **SCRUBBING BRUSH** – for stone and slate floors

1 **DUSTPAN AND BRUSH** – get a good quality one as a cheap one may have a curvy edge which is useless

1 **PACK OF MICROFIBRE CLOTHES** – although rags are perfectly adequate most of the time, microfibre cloths are brilliant for emergency wipe downs especially on paintwork and surfaces, *and* they cut right down on detergent use, which is good for everyone except the manufacturers of detergents

1 **LONG-HANDLED WOOLLEN OR FEATHER DUSTER** – for the cobwebs

1 **FLUFFY DUSTER** – for nooks, crannies and complicated surfaces. Especially good for books

OLD TOOTHBRUSHES – for those awkward bits round taps, plugholes and fittings

WASHING UP BRUSH, SCOURING SPONGES, BOTTLE BRUSH – for washing up

A **BIT OF WIRE WOOL** – for when life is just too short to faff about

A **GOOD LOO BRUSH THAT'S EASY TO CLEAN WITH AND BE CLEANED** – nobody wants to use a scuzzy bog brush

A **BOX OR BASKET WITH A HANDLE** – to carry your cleaning stuff around the house

RUBBER GLOVES AND A TUBE OF HAND CREAM – so your tiny paws are not roughened by work

A **SMALL STEP** – much safer than stretching up or balancing on the sofa

A **PLUNGER** – for those unpleasant blockages

Article from *Housewife Magazine*; 1941

HOUSEHOLD LINEN

It may seem like a simple thing, but not having enough of everything can cause an enormous amount of work when everyone is already busy enough. If you only have one set of bed linen and someone in the house vomits all over it, you're going to be in a pickle. Ditto bedwetters and cocoa spillers (you know who you are …). Likewise, having 10,000 bath sheets donated by well-meaning relatives is an equal burden and there are only so many hair-dye soiled towels you can cut up for floor cloths.

I would recommend the following *per person*:

Bed linen
2 COMPLETE SETS of duvet cover, bottom sheet, pillow cases (2 for single, 4 for double)
1 MATTRESS COVER – essential. Mattresses are expensive and soon ruined by unpleasant fluids

Towels
1 set of bath sheet, large towel, hand towel and 2 flannels

They don't have to all be out at once but you must allow for the sopping wet ones left on the floor and those in the wash.

Also allow about half a dozen old towels for mopping up, extra cover for bedwetters and vomiters and for rubbing down soggy pets/muddy children.

In the Kitchen

8 TEA TOWELS – these must be washed regularly and ideally ironed to kill germs
3 HAND TOWELS
2 TABLECLOTHS – one practical wipe-clean one and one fancy one for entertaining
12 DISHCLOTHS – these can be made from old towels to save money

A Basic First Aid Kit

It is important to have a well-stocked first aid kit in your home to deal with minor accidents and injuries. Everyone in the house should know where it is and I would strongly encourage you to teach your children some basic first aid skills or at least what to do in an emergency. You could be the injured person.

Personally, I would suggest schools teach a little less 'Citizenship' and a bit more cookery, needlework and first aid. But what do I know.

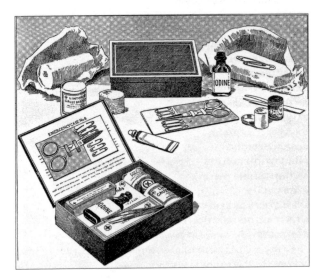

From *The Book of the Home*; 1925. Still relevant, although I would probably leave out the recommended enema syringe …

Remember

Your first aid kit should be locked and kept in a cool, dry place, out of reach of children. Medicines should be checked regularly to make sure that they are reasonably within their use-by dates.

You should also keep a small first aid kit in the car for emergencies.

A basic first aid kit should contain:

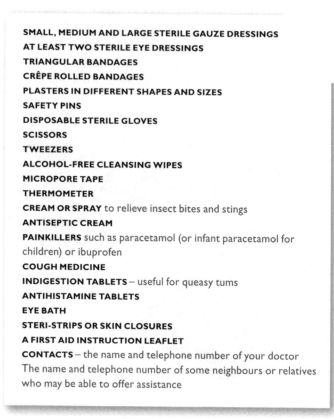

SMALL, MEDIUM AND LARGE STERILE GAUZE DRESSINGS
AT LEAST TWO STERILE EYE DRESSINGS
TRIANGULAR BANDAGES
CRÊPE ROLLED BANDAGES
PLASTERS IN DIFFERENT SHAPES AND SIZES
SAFETY PINS
DISPOSABLE STERILE GLOVES
SCISSORS
TWEEZERS
ALCOHOL-FREE CLEANSING WIPES
MICROPORE TAPE
THERMOMETER
CREAM OR SPRAY to relieve insect bites and stings
ANTISEPTIC CREAM
PAINKILLERS such as paracetamol (or infant paracetamol for children) or ibuprofen
COUGH MEDICINE
INDIGESTION TABLETS – useful for queasy tums
ANTIHISTAMINE TABLETS
EYE BATH
STERI-STRIPS OR SKIN CLOSURES
A FIRST AID INSTRUCTION LEAFLET
CONTACTS – the name and telephone number of your doctor
The name and telephone number of some neighbours or relatives who may be able to offer assistance

The Complementary First Aid Kit

Along with your standard first aid equipment, I would recommend keeping a few bottles of essential oil in the medicine box at all times. These are the concentrated essences of plants obtained predominantly by distillation, and these are available from all good health food shops and quite a lot of chemists these days. Just make sure that they are 100% pure and

"Thanks, Mr. Brown, that'll be all right"

After all, when you can't make the particular dish you first had in mind, there are countless ways to make up, and give you meals just as simple, just as nourishing, just as cheap; and perhaps even nicer.

Potatoes, in particular, help provide a variety of appetising and substantial meals and lend themselves to almost every kind of cooking.

Menu Blues fade away

Carrots are another grand standby. Both potatoes and carrots are health-giving, nourishing and endlessly helpful, from breakfast's start to supper's finish—not only with meat and fish but in salads, and even in puddings or as meals in themselves. You can prove it with the tempting treats printed in the next column.

Full recipes for these or other attractive dishes are given in Food Facts Announcements in the newspapers and the Kitchen Front Talks at 8.15 every morning. Or please send a post-card for them to Room 69F, Ministry of Food, London, S.W.1

BAKEHOUSE MUTTON
Breast of mutton and potato baked together in a simple but unusual way. A very appetising and economical meal.

PIGS IN CLOVER
A novel way with baked potatoes and sausage—a real meal in itself.

CARROT AND POTATO PANCAKE
Just well-seasoned mashed potato with cooked carrot; pan-fried.

CARROT FLAN
Reminds you of apricot flan—but has a deliciousness all its own.

POTATO DROP SCONES
These make a simple sweet for children if served with a spoonful of jam or honey.

Try this one now!

SWEET POTATO PUDDING
Mash 8 oz. cooked potatoes with 1 tablespoon cooking fat, 1 tablespoon honey, and ½ teaspoon salt. Add an egg well beaten and two sticks of rhubarb, cut in dice. Bake in a fireproof dish in a moderate oven for about 45 minutes.

The Ministry of Food, London, S.W.1.

Ministry of Food leaflet

if you are in any doubt as to their use, consult your chemist or a qualified practitioner.

Lavender

This is the all round good egg of the natural pharmacy. It is antiseptic, antifungal, antibiotic and antiviral. It promotes healing particularly for burns and it also helps to reduce scarring, it's calming, helps reduce headaches and promotes deep sleep.

Burns and scalds – put a drop or two directly onto the burn every day until it heals. Remember, if the burn is over 2in, consult a doctor.

Cuts and grazes – clean the wound and the area round it with 5 drops in a small bowl of warm water. Then put one drop neat onto the wound.

Sleep – 10 drops in the bath water will help to promote quiet sleep, also add one drop to the pillow or sheet. For babies, put 1 drop in the bath water and 1 drop on the cot sheet.

Mild shock – if you've had a minor accident or injury, a drop or two of lavender oil either onto the skin or on to clothes near the head is very beneficial in alleviating distress and has a very calming effect in adults and children.

Tea Tree

Another powerful antiseptic and a very effective antifungal. Use for any fungal infections such as athletes foot by putting 10 drops in the bath or a foot bath.

For an ointment use 5 drops mixed thoroughly with zinc and castor oil cream or put 2 drops on a cotton wool ball and smear it on the affected area.

An emergency treatment for vaginal thrush is to mix very thoroughly one drop of oil in 1 tablespoon of zinc and castor oil cream and apply ½ a teaspoon of the cream to the end of a tampon, use a little to rub gently on external areas. This cream also works for the gentleman's area.

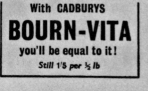
Advertisement from *Housewife Magazine*; 1943

Peppermint

This is excellent for the digestion, is also antiseptic, anti-inflammatory and very cooling. *Indigestion, flatulence, diarrhoea, nausea* – 2 drops in a pint of hot water. Sip this slowly until it is all gone. If it is not relieved in an hour or so, do it again (the vapour will initially make your eyes water a bit – keep them closed).

Tired feet – put 4 drops in a bowl of lukewarm water and soak your feet.

Bad breath – mix 4 drops in a tablespoon of brandy, gin or vodka. Add to a small tumbler of warm water and use as a mouthwash.

Eucalyptus

This is well known for its usefulness with colds, coughs and sinus problems but is also a useful cradle cap remedy, insect repellent and deodorant.

Colds, stuffy noses – put 5 drops in a bowl of very hot water and inhale deeply for at least 10 minutes, making sure that you keep your eyes closed. Put a drop on your handkerchief or tissues as well.

Cradle cap – mix 2 drops in a tablespoon of olive oil and rub very gently into the affected area, taking care to avoid the soft fontanelle at the front of the head.

Also make use of items from your basic store cupboard:

BICARBONATE OF SODA AND VINEGAR for bee and wasp stings:
  Bees = Bicarbonate
  Wasps = Vinegar
HONEY
LEMON JUICE

A Basic Tool Kit

Nobody should be afraid of doing a bit of DIY and everyone should have a few basic tools, whether they're beautiful vintage ones or shiny pink flowery numbers. Whatever type of kit you have, always remember to clean and dry your tools before putting them away or they will rust and become useless.
I would recommend:

A BOX OR BAG in which to keep your tools
A CLAW HAMMER – for hammering and extracting nails
A GOOD SET OF SCREWDRIVERS – including both Philips (cross head) and Pozidriv (single slot)
A BRADAWL – for making starter holes before you screw
A DECENT TAPE MEASURE
A COUPLE OF PENCILS
A PAIR OF PLIERS WITH A WIRE CUTTING BIT
A BOXED SET OF ASSORTED SCREWS, RAWLPLUGS AND NAILS
A SMALL SET OF SPANNERS
A SMALL CAN OF OIL such as WD40
STURDY SCISSORS
A RETRACTABLE STANLEY KNIFE

▼

► **A SMALL SPIRIT LEVEL**

A JUNIOR HACKSAW

A SET OF ASSORTED PAINTBRUSHES

MASKING TAPE

GAFFER TAPE

STRING

A PACK OF ASSORTED SANDPAPER

CLEAR INSTRUCTIONS as to where you've put the first aid kit

A STEPLADDER

A TORCH

A Car Safety/Emergency Kit

Even the newest car can go wrong; some total incompetent can crash into you or the weather can turn nasty and leave you stranded. Be prepared so you can mitigate the worst. As a minimum you should have:

A LONG HANDLED WRENCH – the feeblest person can get wheel nuts off with one of these

SPARE WHEEL in good condition

SOCKET SET

HAMMER

DUCK TAPE

JUMP LEADS

TORCH

SPARE BULBS

A REFLECTIVE WARNING TRIANGLE

Also:

> **FIRST AID KIT**
> **BLANKETS**
> **NOTEBOOK AND PEN**
> **MOBILE PHONE/CAMERA**
> **A HIGH VISIBILITY JACKET**
> **ROAD MAP** – sat navs are only as good as their battery life
> **CEREAL BARS, CHOCOLATE**
> **BOTTLED WATER** and, if you're going on a longer journey, a thermos of hot tea or cocoa
> **A WHISTLE**

GARDEN BASICS

Even if you only have a small garden or are not much of a gardener, you will need a few things to keep it nice. It doesn't have to win awards at Chelsea, but a tidy garden is a pleasant place to be and will convince the neighbours that you are not a complete scuzzer.

Always make sure that you clean and dry your tools after use and put them away in a dry place. They will last you much longer that way.

Essential Tools

> **A LAWNMOWER OF AN APPROPRIATE SIZE TO YOUR GARDEN** – if your lawn is cut, the garden immediately looks better
> **A TROWEL AND FORK** – for planting and weeding
> **A WATERING CAN** – even if you have a hose, sometimes it's more convenient to just grab the can and water something critical. If you want to treat or feed anything, it's much more convenient to use the can

▼

► **A HOSE THAT ATTACHES TO THE OUTSIDE TAP AND CAN BE ROLLED UP TO KEEP IT TIDY** – a hose that lurks about in the undergrowth will soon get flattened or cut to pieces by the mower

A FEW BAMBOO CANES – tie taller plants to canes to stabilise them

STRING – you can never have too much string in any aspect of your life

A PAIR OF GOOD SECATEURS – for cutting tough stalks and twigs. Incidentally this tool is pronounced 'seck-a-turs'. Faulty pronunciation gives you potato blight

A PAIR OF SHEARS – for quick trimming of hedges and shrubs

SLUG PELLETS – stuff beer traps, the slugs must die. They eat your stuff

A WHEELBARROW – or one of those bags you can carry round to put weeds and debris in

GOOD POSTURE – crouching over flower beds can knacker your back, so remember to hold that core!

ACCESS TO A HOT BATH – nothing gets the mud and weevils off you like a good soak.

HOW TO MANAGE STAFF

Very few people maintain a full staff these days, but many employ cleaners, gardeners, home helps, *au pairs* etc. and I hear a great many complaints from both sides of the mop.

Here are some top tips on managing and *keeping* the people you pay to help you. This may seem like an awful lot to think about and some of it may not be relevant, but it is important to get it right. I know people who have had the same home help for forty years and other people who have stormed out after a week because their employer is unrealistic and high-handed.

Find out what people in your area are paid and keep to roughly that figure; too far under and you'll get rubbish applicants, too far over and it's not fair on other people.

Ask for character references and take them up. You are letting a stranger into your home and you will probably need to give them a key; you need to know they are genuine and honest. If they are looking after your children at any time and are not previously known to you, make sure you get a CRB check as well.

Sit down and think very hard about what you actually want doing and then actually do those jobs (if possible). This will give you an idea of how much time you will need someone to work.

Be realistic about what someone can do. You can't expect someone to clean your house from top to bottom, or instantly transform your garden in three hours a week.

Think carefully about what sort of person you want and be realistic. If you live in a four-storey house, a 70-year-old fat person with asthma may not be able to manage the stairs. Likewise if there's heavy work to do in the garden, a skinny 13 year old may also be unsuitable. Trust your instincts – this person may be coming to your house frequently and you need to get on together.

When you interview the person, take them on a tour of the areas for which they will be responsible and make sure they understand the scope of their work.

Always make sure your instructions are clear and demonstrate new tasks if necessary. Cleaning silver or dealing with new plants are good examples of this.

If you are not going to be there when the person is working, leave a list of tasks, at least until you have both established a routine.

Remember that if a comprehensive job is being done, it may take around six months before the person is completely *au fait* with what needs to be done.

Find out if they have other commitments which might impinge on the time they are giving you.

Make it clear that you expect punctuality and reliability. You're not employing them as a favour, you need a job of work done. If they are constantly cancelling or failing to turn up with no explanation, they are no good to you. However, crises occur in everyone's lives and if they have usually proven themselves to be reliable, you must be flexible and understanding.

Have a trial period, for both your sakes.

Make sure that your relationship boundaries are clear – it's very hard to tell someone off or broach a difficult subject if you have become best mates. If you are employing a friend or family member, discuss this eventuality before they start.

Try to create a pleasant atmosphere; if someone is frightened of you or fears ridicule, they are less likely to ask a necessary question. Keep lines of communication open.

Make sure the house is tidy before asking someone to clean it. If they have to tidy up first, the cleaning will not get done.

Let them know if you have any unusual habits or pet hates *before* they get it wrong.

Always pay your help on time and in the manner they are expecting. A cheque is no good to someone who relies on cash on a day to day basis. Discuss with them how they wish to be paid, whether it is daily, weekly etc. and stick to it.

Once you are both happy with each other, consider giving them holiday pay on a pro rata basis. If they work six hours a week, offer them six hours of paid holiday a year. This will generate good will and loyalty.

3

KNITTING, SEWING AND MENDING

Sewing and mending are life skills not optional extras. In order to make the most of your garments and fabrics, you need to know how to turn up a hem, sew on a button or darn the hole in that favourite jumper that got snagged on next door's rambling roses.

I know people who have put a shirt in the bin because it lost a button. This is not only shamefully incompetent, it is also wasteful and wicked. At the very least it should have gone to the charity shop and at best have the button replaced and the life of the shirt extended. If it was truly beyond use, then it could have been made into a child's painting overall or cut up for rags – shirts are brilliant for windows and polishing silver.

No one's asking you to run up a tailored suit or smock a frock, just start off with the basics and you'll be amazed at how satisfying it is to have the skill.

KNITTING

Like so many things, knitting is about knowing the language and understanding the basic techniques. Once you can produce a passable basic stitch, at the very least you can knit a scarf or a patch for a torn jumper. Give it a go is my advice. You may chose not to knit but at least you know you can; when the power goes there'll be no five quid jumpers from Bangladesh and you will be ahead of the game.

GIRL AT THE AWKWARD AGE

By Ann Page. The chrysalis stage, from 14 to 17, halfway between hoyden and charming young woman

Well-Tailored Utility Suit in blue checked tweed. From a group at Swan and Edgar

Advertisement from *Housewife Magazine*.

Abbreviations

k	knit plain
p	purl
st	stitch
sts	stitches
rep	repeat
*	repeat section (a * will appear at the beginning and end of the section to be repeated)
tog	together
st.st	stocking stitch
inc	increase or increasing
dec	decrease or decreasing
beg	beginning
sl	slip (this means transference of a stitch from the left-hand needle to the right-hand needle without knitting it. This is often done in the making of fancy patterns)
pw	purlwise
kw	knitwise
m	make
rib	ribbed fabrics are a combination of plain and purl stitches forming vertical ridges which have the effect of contracting the width of the work while retaining the basic size. Simple ribs such as k1 p1 and k2 p2 are the most commonly used for welts, neckbands etc.

The Different Stitches

Making a stitch by the wool forward method.

Wool round needle.

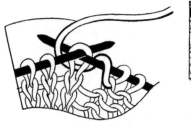

Wool over needle.

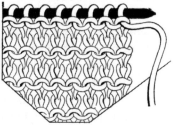

Knitting in garter stitch.

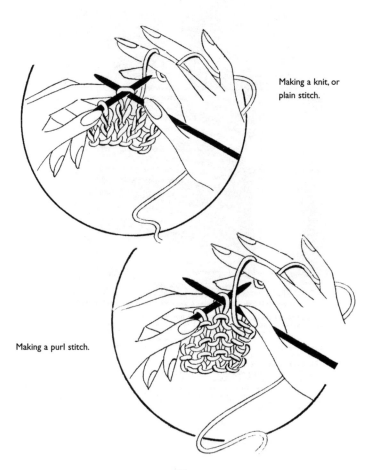

Making a knit, or plain stitch.

Making a purl stitch.

Fair Isle Sleeveless Sweater

Men and women alike look fabulous in a Fair Isle pullover. Worn over a cotton shirt they can brighten up the dullest suit for work wear and look extremely jolly with jeans, cords or chinos. I've been trying to find one for a friend and the cheapest one I came across was over £80 and I've seen them in boutiques for over £200! Be smart – get knitting!

PATONS BEEHIVE FINGERING, 4-ply—"PATONISED," SHRINK RESISTANT

To fit 36-38 inch chest .... Length from top of shoulder .... 24 ins.

| Ground Shade .. 4 ozs. | Banana .... 1 oz. | Yellow .... 1 oz. | Gold .... 1 oz. |
| Navy .. .. 1 oz. | Royal .... 1 oz. | Mid-Blue .... 1 oz. | |

Small quantities Light Blue and Bottle Green.

Knitting Needles, 1 pair each Nos. 9 and 12, 1 set of four No. 12, measured on a Beehive Needle Gauge. Stitch Holder.

ABBREVIATIONS:—See page 17.

TENSION:—To get these measurements it is absolutely necessary to work at a tension to produce 7½ stitches to the inch in width on No. 9 Needles.

Note:—Do not weave colours in Fair Isle pattern, but carry loosely across back of work. It is important, however, that no colour should be stranded over more than 5 sts., and where it has to lie across more than 7 sts., it should be woven over and under 5th and 6th sts. to prevent long loops on back of work.

Fair Isle sweater knitting pattern

The Fair Isle portions of this Pullover are knitted in stocking stitch.

Work repeat of rows 1-58 inclusive from chart throughout, noting that the 18 sts. repeat is worked across row, and that each odd st. is worked once only at end of K. row and beginning of P. row.

THE FRONT:
Using No. 12 Needles and Ground Shade, cast on 124 stitches.

Work in K.2, P.2 rib for 3¼ ins.
In next row.—K.2, (increase in next st., rib 5), twenty times, increase in next st., P.1. (145 sts.)
Change to No. 9 Needles, and proceed in Fair Isle pattern from chart as directed, until work measures 15 ins. from beg., finishing at end of a P. row.
Keeping pattern correct, shape armholes and divide for neck as follows:—
In next row.—Cast off 10, pattern 61 (there now being 62 sts. on needle after cast off), leave these sts. on stitch holder, cast off 1, pattern to end.
In next row.—Cast off 10, pattern 61 (there now being 62 sts. on needle after cast off).
Proceed on these 62 sts. as follows:—
Keeping pattern correct, dec. 1 st. at armhole edge on next and every alt. row, until 9 dec. have been completed at armhole edge, at same time dec. 1 st. at neck edge on next and every 3rd row, until armhole dec. are completed.
Continue dec. at neck edge only on every 3rd row from previous dec., until 36 sts. remain.
Continue on these sts., until work measures 8½ ins. from beg. of armhole shaping, finishing at armhole edge.
Shape shoulder by casting off 12 sts. at beg. of next and every alt. row, until all sts. are cast off. Join in wool, and work on remaining sts. to correspond with other side.

THE BACK.—Work as Front, until armhole shaping is reached.
Keeping pattern correct, shape armholes by casting off 10 sts. at beg. of next 2 rows, dec. 1 st. at both ends of next and every alt. row, until 109 sts. remain.
Continue on these sts., until armholes measure same as Front armholes.
Cast off 12 sts. at beg. of next 6 rows. Cast off.

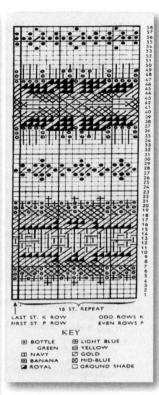

18 ST. REPEAT

LAST ST. K ROW   ODD ROWS K
FIRST ST. P ROW   EVEN ROWS P

KEY

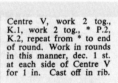

▣ BOTTLE GREEN	⊞ LIGHT BLUE
⊡ NAVY	⊟ YELLOW
▨ BANANA	☒ GOLD
▧ ROYAL	⊠ MID-BLUE
	▢ GROUND SHADE

THE ARMHOLE BANDS.
—Using a back stitch seam, join shoulders of Back and Front.

Using two No. 12 Needles and Ground Shade, with right side of work facing knit up 160 sts. round armhole.

Work in K.2, P.2 rib for 1 in. Cast off in rib.

Work other Armhole Band in same manner.

THE NECK BAND.—Using set of No. 12 Needles and Ground Shade, with right side of work facing, commencing at top of left shoulder, knit up 76 sts. to cast-off st. at Centre V, knit up st. through cast-off st. at Centre V, then knit up 116 sts. to left shoulder. (193 sts.)

Proceed as follows:—

1st round.—* P.2, K.2, repeat from * to last 2 sts. from st. knitted up at Centre V, work 2 tog., K.1, work 2 tog., * P.2, K.2, repeat from * to end of round. Work in rounds in this manner, dec. 1 st. at each side of Centre V for 1 in. Cast off in rib.

TO MAKE UP PULLOVER.—With a slightly damp cloth and warm iron, press lightly. Using a flat seam for ribbing and an ⅛ of an inch back stitch seam for other seams, sew up side seams. Finally, press all seams.

Knit your own Vest and Pants Set

I believe it is the Norwegians who say, 'There is no such thing as bad weather, only inappropriate clothing,' and I concur. I remember at boarding school it was so bloody cold that I bought two pairs of old lady's long knickers from the charity shop to wear over my own. They were harlequin patterned in

THE VEST

Front and Back (both alike).—With No. 4 needle cast on 100 sts. by thumb method.

Now work in g.st. (each row k.) for ½ in., using 1 No. 12 and 1 No. 4 needle.

Continue in st.st. (1 row k., 1 row p.) until the work measures 14 ins. from commencement, ending with a p. row.

Next row.—* K. 4, k. 2 tog., k. 4; rep. from * to end of row (90 sts.).

Using 2 No. 12 needles work 5 ins. in k. 1, p. 1 rib.

Using 1 No. 12 and 1 No. 4 needle work 5 ins. in st.st.

Using 2 No. 12 needles work 1 in. in k. 1, p. 1 rib.

Cast off loosely.

Work the other piece in the same way.

Make-up.—Press work lightly on wrong side, using a hot iron over a damp cloth. Join side seams.

Sew on ribbon in required position for shoulder straps. Press all seams.

THE PANTIES

The Front.—With No. 4 needle cast on 54 sts. by the thumb method.

Using 1 No. 12 and 1 No. 4 needle work in g.st. for ½ in., then continue in st.st. for 1 in., ending with a p. row.

Leave these sts. on a spare needle.

Work another piece in the same way.

Now join the two pieces thus: k. 54 sts., cast on 26 sts. for the gusset, then k. 54 sts. from the spare needle (134 sts.).

Next row.—P.

Shape the Gusset thus :—

1st row.—K. 53, k. 2 tog., k. 24, k. 2 tog., k. 53.

2nd and each alternate row.—P.

3rd row.—K. 53, k. 2 tog., k. 22, k. 2 tog., k. 53.

5th row.—K. 53, k. 2 tog., k. 20, k. 2 tog., k. 53.

Continue decreasing in this way, knitting 2 sts. tog. at each side of the gusset on the next row and on every alternate row until 108 sts. remain, the last row being k. 53, k. 2 tog., k. 2 tog., k. 53.

Next row.—P.

Continue in st.st. without shaping until the work measures 12½ ins. from commencement, ending with a p. row.

Now using 2 No. 12 needles, work in k. 1, p. 1 rib for 3 ins.

Cast off loosely in rib.

The Back.—Work as given for the front until the work measures 12½ ins. from commencement, ending with a p. row.

Shape the Back thus:—

1st row.—K. 58, turn.

2nd row.—P. 8, turn.

3rd row.—K. 13, turn.

4th row.—P. 18, turn.

5th row.—K. 23, turn.

6th row.—P. 28, turn.

Continue in this way, working 5 sts. extra on every row until the sts. are all wo ked on to one needle.

Now using 2 No. 12 needles work in k. 1, p. 1 rib for 3 ins.

Cast off loosely in rib.

Make-up.—Press work lightly on the wrong side, using a hot iron over a damp cloth.

Join side, leg and gusset seams.

Thread the elastic through the waist ribbing (see RINGING THE CHANGES—ACCESSORIES).

Press all seams.

Vest and panties set pattern

scarlet and royal blue and my goodness they kept the draughts from blowing up a girl's tunic! But how much more glamorous would I have been in this beautiful ensemble.

I'm a big believer in wearing more clothes and turning the heating down. This not only stimulates the retail economy but will also lower the nation's energy consumption, and by knitting this yourself, you are provided with cheap entertainment, the deep satisfaction of producing something tangible and practical, and you also have a pair of warm drawers at the end of it. Start your own eco-revolution – wearing woollen underwear.

Vest and Pants Set – Slim-fitting Undies in the Softest Wool!

MATERIALS:
5oz 2-ply wool
1 No.4 and 2 No.12 knitting needles
A fine crochet hook

24in/62cm ribbon
3–4 yards/m fine elastic

MEASUREMENTS:
The vest: Length 25in/64cm
Bust size: 32–36in/82–92cm
The pants: Length from waist to crutch 14in/36cm
Width to widest part: 36in/92cm
Tension: 6 sts to 1in/2.5cm

NB: The vest and pants are worked in st. st. with 1 No.12 and 1 No.4 knitting needles, with the exception of the ribbing.

The vest and panties set in action

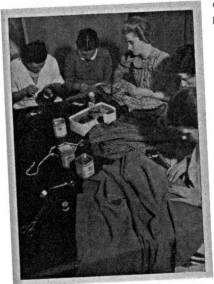

Organise a mending party!

SEWING AND MENDING TECHNIQUES

Sewing is a life skill not an optional extra. The ability to sew on a button, patch some trousers or repair a hem should not be greeted with uproarious applause, because everyone should be able to do it. The applause should be reserved for making a garment last longer and thereby reducing waste and saving you money. For example, whilst I recognise that we are all very busy and that five pairs of socks can be purchased for practically nothing from certain stores, a decent pair of cotton or woollen socks makes the feet less sweaty and will last longer, particularly if you darn any small holes.

The ability to sew on a button also means that you could change the look of a garment by replacing the buttons. I did this with a worn but modern wool coat by replacing the buttons with 1930s ornamental jet buttons. The coat was immediately 'lifted' and still looks good after more than ten years.

So here are some basic sewing stitches to get you going:

RUNNING STITCH – this would be used as the simplest stitch to hold two pieces of material together when the hold doesn't have to be that strong.

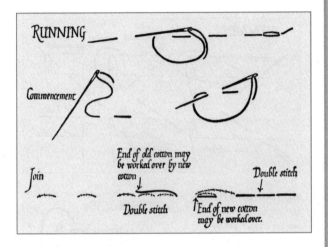

TACKING STITCH – this would be used to hold material in place before machining or careful hand stitching.

BACK STITCHING – this is a strong hand stitching method for firmly attaching two pieces whilst looking like a less obvious running stitch.

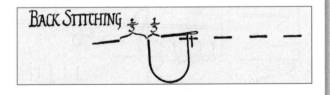

HEMMING STITCH — this is incredibly useful for turning up the hem of a garment so that the fabric hangs correctly but the stitches aren't visible from the right side.

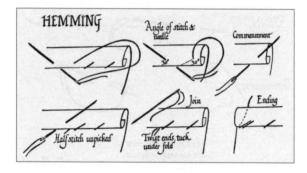

BUTTONHOLE STITCH — garments are often rendered useless by a buttonhole fraying or tearing. It is a tiny stitch which takes a bit of concentration but it's well worth it to save a favourite shirt or jacket.

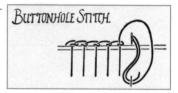

BLANKET STITCH — blanket stitch, as its name suggests, is a technique for securing a raw edge or as a decorative or neatening finish on a piece of work.

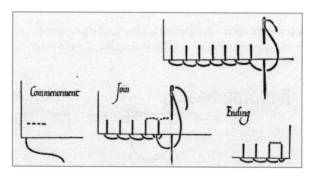

And here are some of the more decorative stitches:

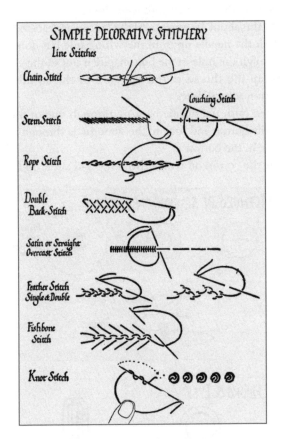

HOW TO SEW ON A BUTTON

- Get some cotton the same colour as the thread on the rest of the buttons
- Thread your needle, then cut a length of cotton about 18in/45cm long
- Tie a couple of knots in the end without the needle on it
- Position the button where you want it and push your needle through one of the holes from the wrong side

- Take the needle back through the other hole, looking to see how the other buttons were done.
- Do this about 10 times until the button appears to be firm
- Push the needle up from the wrong side but don't put it through the hole in the button, pull it out to the side
- Wrap the thread round the core of thread under the button several times
- Then push the needle back up through one of the holes in the button and back to the wrong side through another hole in the button
- Tie the cotton off with a firm knot and cut it off neatly.

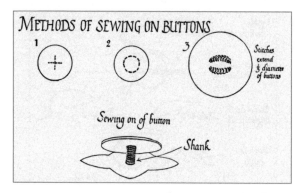

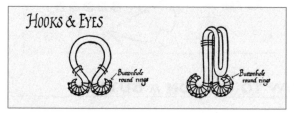

The hook and eye, another fastening method explained

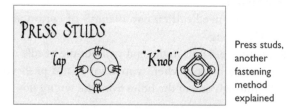

Press studs, another fastening method explained

How to Repair or Make a Buttonhole

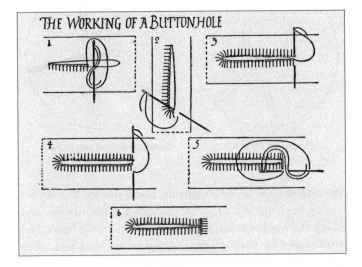

THE WORKING OF A BUTTONHOLE

BASIC CROCHET STITCHES

Crochet is a needlework technique using a crochet hook plus yarn, but all sorts of materials can be used to do interesting and innovative work, even wire, twine or paper.

Crochet is often confused with knitting because they do share similarities, both in their utensils and in the projects which can be created, but it differs from knitting in that only one stitch is being worked at a time, the stitches are usually taller and a single hook is used instead of two needles.

Chain – make a slip knot and place on the hook. Then commence by holding the hook in the right hand and the thread between the thumb and first finger of the left hand – held out taut between the second and third fingers and looped under the little finger – then pass the hook under the thread and pull through. Continue in this way making loops until a sufficient length is made.

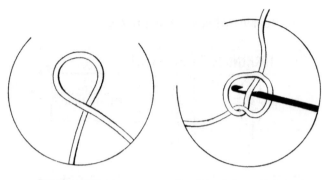

Beginning a slip knot.

Completing the knot with the hook.

Slip stitch or single crochet – insert the hook into the foundation, hook under the thread, draw through the foundation into which the hook was inserted, and the loop on the hook. This stitch is used for passing from one part of the work to another and is practically invisible to the pattern.

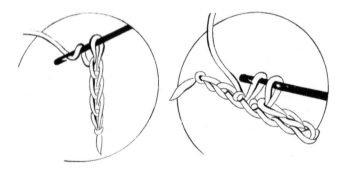

Drawing the wool through the loop.

Slip stitch, or single crochet.

Double crochet – to work double crochet into knitting or crochet, begin with a slip knot (*see above*) ★, put the hook into the foundation, hook under thread, draw through foundation, hook under thread and draw through both loops on the hook.

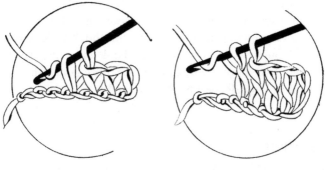

Making a double crochet.   Making a treble.

Treble crochet – to make a treble, with a loop already on the hook ★ hook under thread, hook into foundation, hook under thread, draw through (there are now three loops on the hook), hook under thread, draw through first two loops on the hook, hook under thread, draw through remaining two loops, repeat from ★ for number required.

Short treble – with a loop already on the hook, ★ hook under thread, hook into foundation, hook under, draw through (three loops now on hook), hook under, draw through all loops on hook. Repeat from ★ for number required.

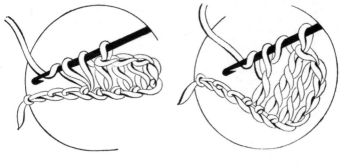

Making a short treble.   Making a long treble.

Long treble – with a loop already on the hook, ★ hook under thread twice, hook into foundation, hook under thread, draw through (four loops are now on the hook), hook under thread, draw through two loops on the hook, hook under thread, draw through two more loops, hook under thread, draw through remaining loops. Repeat from ★ for number required.

CROCHETED

Tea Cosy

MATERIALS
4 oz. 4-ply wool. (Original used 2 oz. maroon, 1 oz. blue and about ½ oz. green.) A medium crochet hook.

MEASUREMENTS
10 ins. by 7 ins.
N.B.—Always turn with 1 ch. at the end of each row.

Side Pieces (two alike).—Using the maroon wool make a chain 10 ins. long.

1st row.—Work in d.c.

2nd row.—Work in d.c. but pick up the vertical st. at the back of previous row each time. Rep. these 2 rows for 7 ins. Fasten off.

Strip for Top and Sides.—Using the blue wool, make a chain 4 ins. long and work in d.c. for 24 ins. Fasten off.

To Make-up.—Using the green wool work a scalloped edging all round each side piece. (*See* RINGING THE CHANGES — DECORATIONS AND ACCESSORIES.) Sew the long strip along three sides. Make a padded lining. (The pieces for the lining should be cut to the shape of the crocheted fabric before making up the cover, leaving about ½ in. on all edges for turnings.) The cover may be lined with felt.

Here is the crocheted cosy, the instructions for which appear on the previous page. Use it for party occasions when there's a crowd.

You can make this simple tea cosy as bright or subtle as you like – perhaps co-ordinate it with your tea set.

DARNING

The important thing to remember about a darn is that it should be as invisible as possible (unless you're deliberately making a feature of it). Make sure that you thread the wool through an unbroken loop at each edge to prevent the hole laddering further. Also copy the tension of the garment when you're weaving the wool through so that it doesn't pull out of shape.

Wrong shape because the strain of the darn comes on the same threads

Methods of darning.

Method of darning across a hole

Crossing a darn near a hole

The darn of the hole on the right side of the garment

Now why not use your newfound darning skills to mend your favourite items?

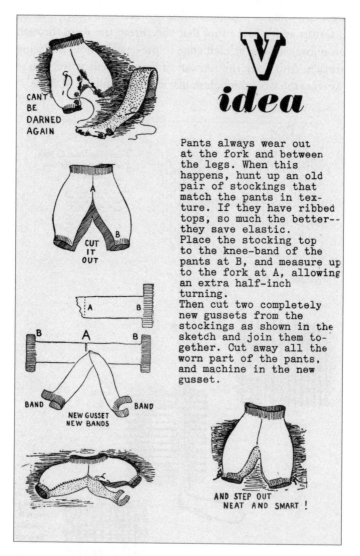

V idea

CAN'T BE DARNED AGAIN

A
B
CUT IT OUT

A B
B A B
BAND BAND
NEW GUSSET NEW BANDS

Pants always wear out at the fork and between the legs. When this happens, hunt up an old pair of stockings that match the pants in texture. If they have ribbed tops, so much the better-- they save elastic. Place the stocking top to the knee-band of the pants at B, and measure up to the fork at A, allowing an extra half-inch turning. Then cut two completely new gussets from the stockings as shown in the sketch and join them together. Cut away all the worn part of the pants, and machine in the new gusset.

AND STEP OUT NEAT AND SMART !

How to mend worn-out pants.

RECIPE SECTION

CONTENTS

All recipes serve 4 unless otherwise stated.

1 Tasmanian Protein on Toast

Tempted as I was to follow the advice of a 1950s Tasmanian* and offer you scrambled sheep's brains, I know my limitations (and yours, I suspect). But as I have pointed out many times, offal is cheap, nourishing and scrumptious. So much offal goes to waste because people have forgotten how to cook it, and we don't like waste. Waste is wicked. Do your bit and eat a kidney.

Oh, and don't worry about a bit of garlic for breakfast, just munch a bit of fresh parsley when you've finished and all will be forgiven.

Utensils
1 frying pan

Ingredients
2oz/60g butter
2 lambs' kidneys – cored and chopped
4 medium-sized button mushrooms – chopped
1 garlic clove – crushed
2 eggs – beaten
Hot buttered toast

Method
Melt the butter in the pan.
Add the kidneys, mushrooms and garlic, and cook over a low heat for about 15 minutes.
Add the beaten egg and cook slowly, stirring continuously until the egg starts to set.
Pile onto hot buttered toast.
Start the day with a spring in your step.

* Not strictly British I know, but doesn't a former colony count?

2   Wartime Housewife's Granola

The most delicious and nutritious breakfast you could ever wish for!

My favourite way of eating granola is with a great dollop of natural yoghurt on the top and a few slices of apple or other fresh fruit. This is a super-powered breakfast or snack that will completely set you up for the day, slowly releasing energy until the next meal.

Utensils

1 ovenproof dish about 8x10in/20x25cm and at least 1½in/
   4cm deep
1 large mixing bowl
1 small mixing bowl
Baking parchment to line the dish
1 metal spatula/fish slice

Ingredients

8oz/240g porridge oats
1 teaspoon cinnamon
½ teaspoon nutmeg
1 teaspoon salt
3 tablespoons sunflower oil
3 generous tablespoons honey
3oz/90g dark brown soft sugar
1 teaspoon vanilla extract
1 ½oz/45g sunflower seeds
1 ½oz/45g flaked almonds
1 ½oz/45g dried cranberries
1 ½ oz/45g raisins

Method

Preheat the oven to 260C/325F/gas mark 3.
Line the ovenproof dish with parchment.
In the large bowl mix together the oats, salt and spices.

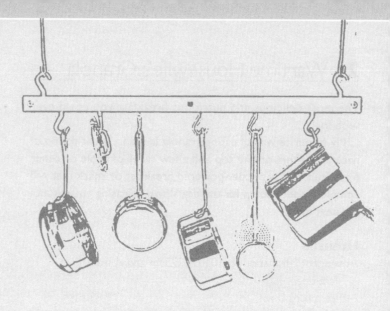

Put the oil, honey, brown sugar and vanilla extract into the
    medium bowl and mix well.

Pour the honey mixture into the oats and mix well with a spoon
    until all the oats are covered with the honey liquid.

Now get your hands in there and really give it a good mix
    and squeeze.

Spoon the mixture into the ovenproof dish squeezing a few bits
    together to get some clusters in there.

Put into the oven and bake for 15 minutes.

Remove from the oven and flip the mixture over with the spatula.

Return to the oven for another 15 minutes.

Remove and leave to cool completely – I usually lift the
    parchment out which lets it cool quicker.

When it is quite cool, mix in the fruit and nuts.

Store in an airtight container.

3   Scotch Woodcock

I like something hot inside me on a cold winter's day and the Victorian **Scotch Woodcock** is a tasty variation on **scrambled eggs** on toast. If you haven't had **Gentleman's Relish** before, it is made from anchovies and is therefore quite salty, so go easy with it at first. I have no idea why it's called 'Scotch Woodcock' any more than I know why a wartime lentil dish could be construed as 'Mock Duck', but that is the joy of British cookery. Believe it or not, this dish would have been served at the end of a multi-course meal. Blimey.

I confess now that I make scrambled eggs in the microwave because I cannot bear washing up eggy pans. You do it just the same as you would in a pan, you just have to keep taking it out and whisking it periodically with a fork to keep it fluffy. You have to watch it quite carefully to make sure it's not overdone, but that's the price one pays for meddling with Satan's Stove. I have never had anything but low, spaniel fawning from people over my scrambled eggs, so don't get sniffy about it.

This recipe serves 2.

Utensils

1 heavy based saucepan or a microwave-safe bowl
1 whisk

Ingredients

4 slices of wholemeal or granary toast – buttered
1 small tub of Gentleman's Relish
4 eggs
1 tablespoon milk
1oz/30g butter
1 tablespoon double cream
A bit of fresh parsley to garnish if you're feeling posh

THE MORE YOU WORK·

the better sleep
you need

*You're not doing your bit if
you're not really fit !*

Here are two 'scientific sleep' tips to try out
to-night. See how much better they make
you feel in the morning!

1 Whatever your worries—*think of something that makes you feel happy for at
   least half-an-hour before bedtime every
   night.* Troubled sleep is unhealthy sleep.

2 Make a 'nightcup' of Bourn-vita a
   regular habit—it will soothe you, help
   digestion and calm your whole body.

*Start taking these two hints to-night—and you'll find
they make a world of difference to your pep and go.*

With CADBURYS
BOURN-VITA

you'll be equal to it !

Still 1/5 per ½ lb

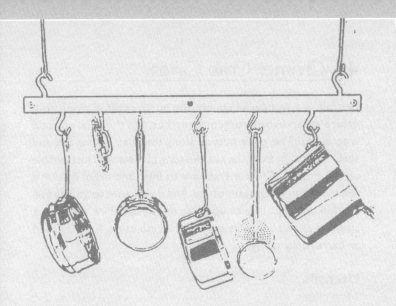

Method

Spread the toast generously with Gentleman's Relish.

Melt the butter with the milk in the saucepan.

Add the eggs and whisk well to blend.

Cook over a low heat, whisking periodically until the egg is just
setting nicely.

Remove from the heat, season with a little black pepper and
whisk in the cream.

Pile onto the toast, garnish if you're going to and serve
immediately.

4 Cromer Crab Cakes

Norfolk is a wonderful county; the north coast is awash with nature reserves and gorgeous beaches, and the local seafood is to die for. There are huts all along the coast selling fish and shellfish straight from the sea, the song of mermaids just audible on the crisp air. Cromer crabs are so fresh and full of flavour it will make you weep tears of joy. And if you want to go The Full Norfolk, attempt to pick up some marsh samphire and have it steamed as an accompaniment to the crab cakes. You may need an extra hanky though.

Utensils
1 fine grater
1 large bowl
1 small bowl
1 large heavy based frying pan
1 baking tray
Cling film
Kitchen roll

Ingredients
1 dressed Cromer crab – with the meat taken out
1 tablespoon fresh parsley – finely chopped
½ teaspoon English mustard
1 teaspoon Worcestershire sauce
2 eggs
1 tablespoon sour cream
½ lemon
2oz/60g wholemeal breadcrumbs
2oz/60g wholemeal plain flour
2 tablespoons vegetable oil

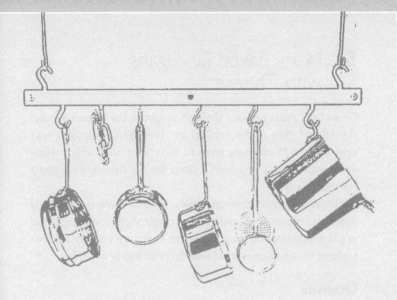

Method

Grate the lemon rind and put 1 teaspoon of the juice to one side.

Mix together the crab meat, parsley, mustard, Worcester sauce, the sour cream, lemon juice and rind, and the yolk of one of the eggs together.

Mix in some breadcrumbs, a little at a time, until the mixture forms a stiff-ish paste.

Form the mixture into small cakes.

Put the flour into a bowl and dip the cakes into it to coat them.

Beat the other egg and dip the crab cakes into it.

Then coat them in the remaining breadcrumbs.

Put the crab cakes onto a lined baking tray, cover with cling film and chill for about an hour.

Remove from the fridge and heat the oil in the frying pan.

Fry for 2–3 minutes on both sides until nicely brown.

Drain on kitchen paper and serve.

5   Manx Baked Tanrogans with Cheese

One of the most popular shellfish caught in the waters around the Isle of Man is the scallop or 'Tanrogan'. Tanrogan was originally the Manx name given to the scallop shell which, when filled with fish oil, provided a lamp for the fishermen, using a rush for the wick.

Miniature scallops, or queenies, have become increasingly popular in recent years and these versatile shellfish are exported in great quantities all over the world. There are roughly a dozen scallops to the lb, compared with forty to eighty queenies.

Utensils
1 sharp knife
1 ovenproof dish
If using scallops keep the shells. If using queenies you will need 4
    suitable heatproof dishes for serving
1 medium saucepan
1 cheese grater

Ingredients
8 scallops or 40 queenies
¼ pint/150ml fish stock
1 small onion, quartered
Salt and pepper
One bay leaf

Method
Pre-heat the oven to 180C/350F/gas mark 4.
Remove scallops from their shells and clean, but do not remove
    the yellow tip.
Place in an ovenproof dish with the stock, onion, seasoning and
    bay leaf.

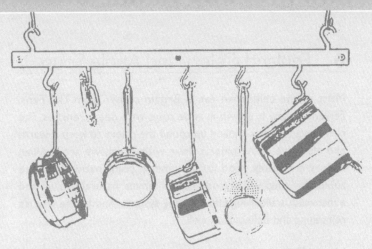

Cover and cook gently in a moderate oven for about 10 minutes.
Lift out the scallops and replace them in their shells, keep the
juice in the dish for use in the sauce.

The Sauce

Ingredients

1oz/30g butter
1oz/30g plain flour
¼ pint/150ml milk
2oz/60g Cheddar cheese – grated
2 tablespoons double cream
A pinch or two of paprika

Method

Melt butter in the pan.
Stir in the flour and cook for 1 minute.
Remove from the heat and gradually add the milk and the liquor
from the scallops, stirring continuously. Bring to the boil.
Beat in cream and half of the grated cheese.
Pour a little of the sauce into each scallop shell and sprinkle with
the rest of the grated cheese.
Sprinkle with a pinch of paprika.
Brown under the grill.

6   Fenland Celery and Apple Soup

Most of the celery we eat in Britain comes from The Fens. Fenland celery is grown in wide rows with deep trenches. The rich Fenland soil is banked up round the celery to keep it warm and also give it the paler colour with which we are familiar. Celery is terribly good for you and, in combination with the apple, this soup will provide fibre, vitamins, natural sodium and a marvellous alkalising effect on the system. And by the way, it's refreshing and delicious as well.

Utensils
1 large saucepan
1 stick blender
1 vegetable peeler

Ingredients
1 onion – finely chopped
1 good knob of butter
4 sticks celery – chopped
2 dessert apples – peeled, cored and chopped
1 pint/600ml chicken or vegetable stock
2 teaspoon fresh or 1 teaspoon dried parsley
2 teaspoon fresh or 1 teaspoon dried mint
A couple of tablespoons double cream or crème fraiche to taste

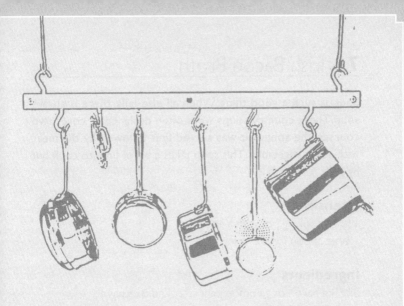

Method

Melt the butter in a pan over a moderate heat.

Add the onion and cook until soft but do not allow to go brown.

Add the celery, apple, parsley and mint and cook for 1 minute.

Add the stock and simmer gently until the celery and apple are soft.

Using the blender, puree until smooth.

Stir in the cream or crème fraiche and serve.

A swirl of cream and a little fresh parsley on top will give it the finishing touch.

7   Irish Bacon Broth

Soup is such a good thing. When all else fails, there is always soup. These country soups were often designed to cover two courses; the soupy bit was served first followed by the meat with some vegetables. This soup takes a bit of time to cook but by golly it's worth it.

Utensils
1 large cooking pot with a lid
1 large spoon for skimming

Ingredients
2lb/1kg bacon or gammon joint – soaked overnight
2oz/60g red lentils
2oz/60g pearl barley
5 medium carrots – sliced
2 medium onions – sliced
2 medium parsnips – peeled and cubed
1 bouquet garni
1lb/500g potatoes – peeled and sliced
1 small cabbage – stalked and quartered
1 leek – sliced
1 tablespoon fresh and chopped or ½ tablespoon dried parsley

Method
Scrape the skin of the bacon joint and place in the pot with just enough water to cover it.
Bring to the boil and skim off any scum that forms on the top.
Add the barley and lentils, bring to the boil, then simmer for about half an hour.
Add the carrots, onions, parsnips, bouquet garni.
Cover the pan and simmer for another half hour.

Add the potatoes and cabbage, bring back to the boil and
    simmer until the potatoes are just soft.
Test the bacon – if it is not cooked through, cook for another
    few minutes until it is.
Five minutes before serving, add the leeks and parsley.
Lift the bacon from the pot, take the skin off then cut it up into
    small chunks and return to the soup.

8   Hampshire Watercress Soup

Watercress is a much underestimated vegetable that is a powerhouse of nutrients. Gram for gram, watercress contains more vitamin C than oranges, more calcium than milk, more iron than spinach and more folate than bananas. It has been grown in Hampshire for generations and the famous railway Watercress Line was established to service the watercress industry. It's good for you, it supports British growers and it tastes delicious. What more do you want?

Utensils
1 large saucepan
1 stick blender

Ingredients
2oz/60g butter
8oz/240g onion – finely chopped
2 garlic cloves – finely chopped
1½lb/750g watercress – tough stalks removed
1¾ pints/1 litre boiling water
Salt and pepper
20 ice cubes
6 floz/175ml crème fraiche

Method
Melt the butter in a large pan and cook the onion and garlic until soft and translucent but not browned.

Turn up the heat, add the watercress and a pinch of salt, cover and cook for 1 minute.

Pour in the boiling water and simmer for 3–4 minutes.

Remove from the heat and add the ice, then leave until the ice has completely melted – this preserves the colour and nutrients of the soup.

Puree with the stick blender.

Just before serving, stir through the crème fraiche.

9   Glamorgan Sausages

The recipe calls for 3 egg yolks, but only 1 egg white – use the remaining egg whites to make meringues for pudding! It's also a great standby for when veggie friends come to tea because it shows you've made an effort and everyone will like them.

Utensils
1 large mixing bowl
1 medium mixing bowl
2 shallow bowls for dipping and rolling
1 whisk
1 large frying pan
Kitchen paper

Ingredients
5oz/150g mature Cheddar cheese – grated
6oz/180g fresh breadcrumbs
2 spring onions – finely chopped
3 egg yolks – have another egg in reserve in case of dryness
1 egg white – beaten
1 tablespoon fresh parsley – finely chopped
1 teaspoon mustard powder
Oil for frying

Method
Mix together the cheese, spring onions and 5oz/150g of the
    breadcrumbs in a large bowl.
In the medium bowl whisk the egg yolks with the parsley and
    mustard.
Add this to the cheese mixture and blend together well.
Season to taste.

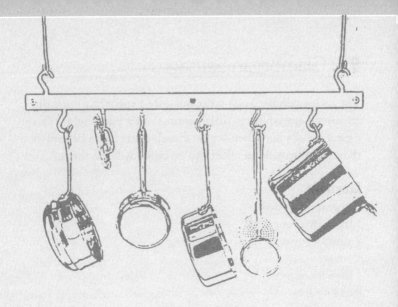

If the mixture is too dry or crumbly to make into shapes, add
   another egg yolk.
Divide the mixture into 12 equal pieces and roll each one into a
   sausage shape about 2in/5cm long.
Dip the sausages into the egg white then roll them in the
   remaining breadcrumbs.
Heat the oil in a large frying pan and fry the sausages, turning
   frequently, until golden brown.
Blot off excess oil on kitchen paper and serve.

10 Northumberland Pan Haggerty

This dish works best with firm fleshed potatoes. The great thing about this is that you can add other bits or leftovers to it to flesh it out, e.g. bacon, cabbage, ground meat etc. Its name is said to come from the French 'hachis' meaning to chop or slice. It is always served straight from the pan and traditionally served with kippers.

Utensils

1 large, heavy frying pan
1 chopping board
1 cheese grater
A grill

Ingredients

4oz/120g butter
1lb/480–500g potatoes – thinly sliced
1 large onion – finely sliced
4oz/120g strong Cheddar cheese – grated
A little black pepper

Method

Heat the butter in the pan over a moderate heat.
Take the pan off the heat and add alternate layers of potatoes, onions and cheese, starting and finishing with potatoes.
Season each layer as you prefer.
Put the pan back on the heat and cook for half an hour until the potatoes are soft.
Lift up the bottom layer to check that it is nicely browned.
Meanwhile, heat the grill.
When it's cooked, place the pan under the grill and cook for a further 5 or 10 minutes to brown off the top.
Cut into wedges and serve straight from the pan.

11   Devonshire Parsnip Fritters

These little fritters can be made in advance and frozen, so great for using up a glut of parsnips or leftovers from the Sunday roast. Their sweet flavour goes beautifully with greasier meats such as roast lamb, duck or goose.

Utensils
1 medium saucepan
1 potato masher
1 large bowl
1 frying pan

Ingredients
4 medium parsnips
4 tablespoons self raising flour
1 medium egg – beaten
A little black pepper
A pinch of turmeric
A little flour for the worktop
Butter for frying

Method
Boil or roast the parsnips until soft and mash them up well.
Put all the ingredients except the butter into a bowl and mix well.
Flour your worktop and divide the mixture into little patties.
Heat the butter in the frying pan.
Fry the fritters on both sides until nicely browned and crispy.
Serve hot.

12   Creamed Spinach

I *love* spinach. Not only does it taste fabulous, but one can also gloat about how much iron and vitamins you're getting. If it's good enough for Popeye, it's good enough for me. Incidentally, young nettles would be just as good in this recipe and they are, of course, free.

Pop a poached egg on the top and you have lunch!

Utensils
1 heavy based saucepan with a lid
1 stick blender

Ingredients
2oz/60g butter
2lb/1kg fresh spinach
3floz/90ml double cream
1 teaspoon lemon juice
Black pepper

Method
Melt the butter in the pan and add the spinach.
Toss it around to coat the spinach in the butter, cover the pan
    and cook for a few minutes.
Remove the lid and cook for another couple of minutes.
Mash up with the blender.
Stir in the cream.
Stir in the lemon juice and grind a bit of black pepper into it.

13   Braised Red Cabbage from Oop North

There can be few vegetable dishes that are as warming and comforting as red cabbage. It goes beautifully with meat but I can quite happily eat a plateful all by itself. It looks gorgeous and smells divine, and is so easy to make.

Utensils
1 large ovenproof dish with a lid

Ingredients
2lb/1kg (approx.) red cabbage – large white ribs removed and finely shredded
2 medium onions – finely sliced
4 dessert apples – peeled, cored & finely chopped
¼ teaspoon ground cinnamon
¼ teaspoon ground cloves
½ teaspoon grated nutmeg
1 tablespoon dark brown sugar
3 tablespoon red wine or cider vinegar
2 tablespoons redcurrant or cranberry or quince jelly
2oz/60g butter

Method
Preheat the oven to 160C/325F/gas mark 3.
Mix all the ingredients together in the dish.
Dot the butter over the top.
Cover the dish and cook for approximately 1½ hours.
Stir a couple of times during cooking.
Serve hot.

14   Suffolk Grumbly

This is one of the most comforting dishes you will ever eat. Served with some colourful vegetables, a jacket potato or chips and a foaming pint of beer and you be comforted and nourished, my children.

Utensils

1 blender or chopper for making breadcrumbs *
1 lasagne-type dish (min. 3in/7cm deep)
1 chopping board
1 cheese grater
1 large mixing bowl
1 medium saucepan

Ingredients

1lb/500g sausage meat
1 medium onion – finely chopped
2oz/60g wholemeal bread crumbs
1 teaspoon mixed herbs
2 eggs
Paprika

Cheese sauce

2oz/60g butter
2oz/60g wholemeal flour (or 2 really heaped tablespoons)
4oz/120g cheese – grated
½ pint/300ml milk
1 pinch mustard powder or ¼ teaspoon readymade mustard

Method

Heat the oven to 180C/350F/gas mark 4.
Melt the butter in a pan then slowly stir in the flour to make thick paste (a roux).
Add the milk a bit at a time, stirring constantly.

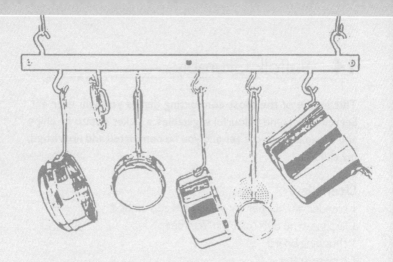

Simmer gently until the sauce has thickened slightly and then stir in the cheese and the mustard.

This sauce needs to be thick or it will slop everywhere when you put the sausagemeat on top.

Mix all the other ingredients together in a bowl – I use my hands and squelch away like billy-oh.

Lightly grease an ovenproof dish and spread half of the sausage mixture in the bottom of the dish.

Pour half of the cheese sauce over the mixture.

Spread the rest of the sausage mixture over that, followed by the rest of the cheese sauce.

Sprinkle liberally with paprika.

Bake in the oven for 1 hour – the top should be well browned.

---

* A word about breadcrumbs

If you are a family who doesn't like its crusts, keep them in a bag in the fridge until you have a few. Using a blender make them into breadcrumbs. Put the crumbs in a sealable bag and put in the freezer until needed. They can then be used to coat chicken or Glamorgan sausages, in brown bread ice cream or as a crunchy top on savoury dishes. Or indeed for a Suffolk Grumbly.

15 Huntingdon Fidget Pie

This pie was originally made around harvest time, to feed the hungry farm hands. Fidget or 'fitchett' pies were once made all over the Midlands, as portable food for working men – in a similar vein to the Cornish pasty or the hot pie of Lancashire. It's lovely served with seasonal vegetables (I like dark green leaves) and a nice sweet purée of swede and carrots.

Utensils
1 rolling pin
1 pie dish (approx 1 pint capacity)
1 chopping board
1 pastry brush
1 small bowl or measuring jug

Ingredients
1 packet shortcrust pastry
8oz/240g lean back bacon – roughly chopped
1 medium onion – chopped
8oz/240g cooking apples – peeled, cored and roughly chopped
1 tablespoon fresh or ½ tablespoon dried parsley
¼ pint/150ml medium cider
1 flat tablespoon plain floor
Egg or milk to glaze

Method
Pre-heat the oven to 190C/375F/gas mark 5.
Mix together the bacon, onion, apples and parsley in the pie dish.
Mix the flour, a little at a time, with the cider into the dish.
Roll out the pastry to about ¼in/½cm thick.
Moisten the edge of the pie dish with water.
Place pastry over the pie dish and trim off any excess.
Make a few slits in the pastry to let the steam out.
Brush the top with beaten egg or milk.
Bake for about 45 minutes or until the pastry is golden brown.

16 Wartime Housewife's Liver in White Wine and Crème Fraiche

I'm a big fan of liver. It's really cheap, very filling, versatile and full of iron. A lot of people are put off offal because they've only ever had it badly cooked. Lamb's and calf's liver is as light as a feather and cuts like butter. Try it, you'll like it.

Utensils
1 large frying pan

Ingredients
2oz/60g butter
1lb/480g liver – tubes cut off and cut into small slices
1 medium onion – finely chopped
1 garlic clove – finely chopped
1 teaspoon fresh or ½ teaspoon dried sage
2 teaspoon fresh or 1 teaspoon dried parsley
¼ pint/150ml white wine
2 full tablespoons crème fraiche (i.e. good dollops)

Method
Heat the butter in the frying pan.
Add the liver and brown slightly, turning as you do so.
Add the onion and garlic and fry until soft but not brown.
Add the wine and herbs, and simmer gently until the liver is
    cooked through.
Add the crème fraiche and heat through, stirring well.
Serve immediately with buttery mashed potatoes and vegetables.

Top tips for tenderness
Soak the liver in milk for an hour or two before cooking. This seems to improve the texture and soften it.
Don't cook it for too long, undercook by preference as this will keep it more tender.

WOMEN!

Farmers can't grow all your vegetables

YOU MUST GROW YOUR OWN

Farmers are growing more of the other essential crops—potatoes, corn for your bread and food for the cows. It's up to *you* to provide the vegetables that are vital to your children's health—especially in winter. Grow all you can. If you don't, they may go short. Turn your garden over to vegetables. Get the older children to help you. If you haven't a garden ask your local council for an allotment. DO IT NOW.

DIG
for Victory

ISSUED BY THE MINISTRY OF AGRICULTURE

17 Irish Pot Roasted Brisket with Guinness

Brisket is a much overlooked cut of beef and, if cooked properly, i.e. long and slow, it provides a cheap and delicious meal. I would suggest doing the 2½ hours of cooking in a slow cooker, then you can forget all about it until suppertime.

Irish beef is some of the best in the world, being beautifully tender and full of flavour whilst a good stout is practically a meal in itself.

The beauty of this particular dish is that the leftovers can provide two further dishes; the meat can go to make beef hash and the vegetables and gravy can be puréed for soup or added to with more vegetables and a few sausages. In fact, with careful planning and assiduous heating, this dish could practically go on indefinitely …

Utensils

1 large casserole dish – suitable for hob top and oven, with a lid

Ingredients

2 tablespoons olive oil
2lb/1kg piece of beef brisket
2 onions – chopped into chunks
3 sticks of celery – chopped into chunks
1lb/480g carrots – chopped into chunks
2lb/1kg potatoes – washed and cut into chunks
2oz/60g plain flour
1 pint/600ml beef stock
½ pint/300ml Guinness (other stouts are available!)
2 bay leaves
3 tablespoons fresh or 1½ tablespoons dried thyme – chopped
2 teaspoons dark muscovado sugar
1 tablespoon tomato purée
1 tablespoon wholegrain mustard

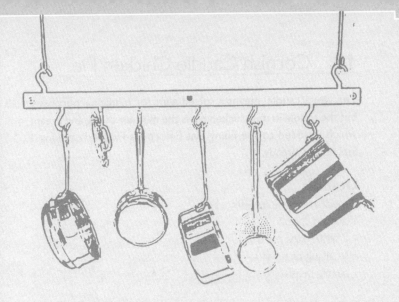

Method

Pre-heat the oven to 180C/350F/gas mark 4.

Heat the oil in the casserole dish until it's sizzling and seal the beef all over.

Remove the beef from the pan and drain off the oil.

Add the onions and cook until soft but not brown.

Now add the celery, carrots and potatoes and cook until the edges are just starting to soften.

Gradually stir in the flour and cook for another minute.

Now gradually pour in the stock and bring to the boil, stirring briskly in a figure of eight motion.

Add the bayleaf, thyme, mustard, sugar and tomato purée and season to taste.

Pop the meat back in the pan, put the lid on and put it in the oven (or transfer to a slow cooker).

Cook for about 2½ hours or until the meat is really tender.

18   Cornish Caudle Chicken Pie

The word 'caudle' means a spiced wine for medicinal purposes, but the caudle in this chicken pie is the mixture of egg and cream which is added to the filling just before it's finished cooking. I feel better already.

Utensils
1 medium saucepan with a lid
1 slotted spoon
1 2 pint/1 litre pie dish
1 small jug or bowl
1 pastry brush

Ingredients
½ oz/15g butter
1 teaspoon sunflower oil
1 medium onion – finely chopped
4 chicken breasts, skinned and chopped
2 tablespoon fresh parsley, chopped or 2 tablespoons dried parsley
4 spring onions – trimmed and chopped
¼ pint/150ml milk
8 oz /250g puff pastry – buy it, life's too short
¼ pint/150ml crème fraiche
2 eggs – beaten

Method
Pre-heat oven to 220C/425F/gas mark 7.

Heat the butter and oil in a frying pan over a moderate heat.

Add the onion, cover and cook until softened but not browned.

Spoon into the pie dish.

Turn up the heat and put the chicken into the pan and cook until evenly browned.

Remove from the pan and place on top of the onion in a single layer.

Put the parsley, spring onions and milk into the pan and bring
slowly to the boil stirring constantly.

Simmer for 2–3 minutes, then pour the sauce over the chicken.

Bake for 30 minutes, until the chicken is tender, then take it out
of the oven and leave to cool.

While the chicken is cooking, roll out the pastry on a lightly
floured surface until it's just a little bit bigger all round than
the pie dish.

Leave the pastry to relax while the filling is cooling.

When cool, moisten the edge of the pie dish then cover with
the pastry.

Fork or crimp the edges to make it look professional and make
a small hole in the top into which you will later pour the eggs
and cream.

Beat the crème fraiche and eggs together and brush the top of
the pie lightly with a bit of the mixture to glaze.

Bake for 15–20 minutes, until nicely browned.

Turn the oven down to 180C/350F/gas mark 4.

Pour the egg and cream mixture through the hole in the top of
the dish.

Return to the oven for about 15 minutes. Cover with foil if the
pastry is browning too quickly.

Remove from the oven and allow to rest for 5 minutes before
serving or leave to cool completely and serve cold.

19   Lancashire Cheese and Butter Pie

Don't be put off by the fact that this dish has the word 'butter' in the title. It is a bit heavy on dairy but fat is not our enemy in moderation – we need it to stay mentally and physically healthy. We used to be given this when we were children and it has been a firm favourite down the generations; I would suggest serving it with dark green vegetables such as broccoli, Savoy cabbage or green beans.

Utensils

1 large mixing bowl
1 large saucepan
1 medium pan
1 medium pie dish
1 colander
1 rolling pin

Ingredients

For the pastry

8oz/240g plain flour
2oz/60g butter
2oz/60g lard (use vegetable fat or dripping if you're too chicken to eat lard)
Ice-cold water

For the filling

3 large potatoes – cut into slices (peeled or not according to taste – I never do)
1 large onion – cut into half slices
2oz/60g butter – cut into very small pieces
4oz/120g for softening the onions
12oz/360g Lancashire cheese – thinly sliced or crumbled

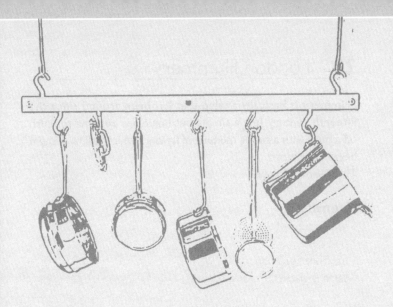

Method

Pre-heat oven to 180C/375F/gas mark 5.

Sift the flour and salt into a bowl and stir in the butter and lard.

Rub in the butter until it resembles fine crumbs.

Gradually add just enough cold water to make the pastry form a ball.

Wrap the dough in cling film and put in the fridge to chill for half an hour.

Parboil the potatoes until they are just soft but still holding their shape.

Cook the onions in the butter until soft and translucent, but not browned.

Roll out about two thirds of the pastry and line the pie dish, trimming the edges.

Drain the potatoes then layer them with the onions, the cheese and butter pieces, seasoning as you go.

Roll out the remains of the pastry and cover and seal it on top of the pie.

Make air vents in the pastry to let out the steam.

Bake for about 30 minutes until the pastry is golden on top.

20   London Flummery

Flummery is basically a whip that has been around since the fifteenth century. It is a simple but luxurious pudding to finish off a meal with a subtle mixture of flavours which will have them begging for more.

This recipe serves 6.

Utensils
1 medium bowl
1 fine sieve
1 medium saucepan
6 serving glasses

Ingredients
4 tablespoons oatmeal soaked in water for 48 hours
6floz/175ml orange juice
2oz/60g caster sugar
¼ pint/150ml double cream

For the top
Finely grated peel of two oranges
4 tablespoons clear honey
2 tablespoons brandy (or whisky if you prefer)
¼ pint/150ml whipped cream
A little crystallised angelica

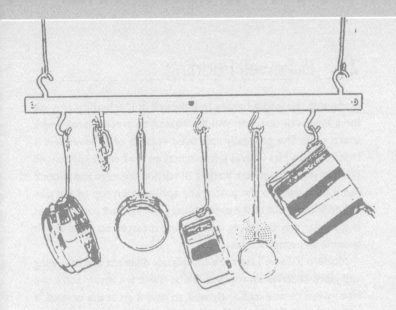

Method

Give the oatmeal a good stir then strain off the liquid into a
medium saucepan.

Throw away the oatmeal or put it out for the birds.

Pour in the orange juice and add the sugar.

Bring to the boil, stirring constantly for approx. 10 minutes or
until the mixture has become very thick.

Allow to cool until nearly cold then fold in the cream.

Spoon into individual glasses and leave to set in a cold place for
about an hour.

Just before serving, sprinkle each pudding with the orange peel,
pour over a little honey, then the brandy.

Then swirl a little whipped cream on the top and decorate with
a little piece of angelica.

21 Bakewell Pudding

If you ever go into a bakery in Bakewell in Derbyshire and ask for a Bakewell tart, you will be treated to steely glares and a sharp reply. The generally approved version of its invention is that in 1820 a Mrs Graves left instructions for her inexperienced cook to make a jam tart. Instead of stirring the eggs and almond paste mixture into the pastry, she spread it on top of the jam. When it came out of the oven, the egg and almond paste had set in a similar way to an egg custard, and it tasted so good that it became an instant success.

Modern Bakewell tarts are completely different and have icing and glacé cherries on top and, whilst these are lovely, someone else makes them exceedingly well, so have a go at the original. It seems like a faff but it really isn't.

Utensils
1 rolling pin
An 8 in/20cm pie dish
Baking beans
Greaseproof paper
1 medium mixing bowl
An electric mixer, or a wooden spoon and some elbow grease
1 fine grater

Ingredients
18oz/500g puff pastry
3 tablespoons raspberry jam
5oz/150g butter
5oz/150g super fine/caster sugar
3 medium eggs plus 1 yolk – beaten
5oz/150g ground almonds
1 lemon – rind grated
2 teaspoon almond essence
1oz/30g flaked almonds
Icing sugar for dusting

Method

Preheat the oven to 190C/375F/gas mark 5.

Lightly flour your work surface and roll out the pastry to ¼in/5mm thick.

Grease and flour the pie dish and line with the pastry.

Prick the base liberally with a fork then chill for 20 minutes.

Cover the pastry lightly with greaseproof paper and fill with baking beans.

Place in the oven and bake for 15 minutes until the pastry is lightly browned.

Take out the baking beans and bake for a further 5 minutes.

Remove from the oven.

Spread the raspberry jam onto the base of the pastry case and set aside.

Cream the butter and sugar until it becomes pale – an electric mixer will do this much more quickly.

Beat the egg yolk into the beaten eggs and then gradually add to the creamed butter and sugar.

Lightly fold in the ground almonds, grated lemon rind and almond extract.

Pour the mixture into the pastry case and smooth the surface evenly.

Bake for 30 minutes.

Remove from the oven, sprinkle on the flaked almonds and return to the oven for a further 10 minutes.

Sprinkle with icing sugar whilst still warm and serve.

A word regarding puff pastry

Of course one can make it from scratch but life is simply too short and I buy it ready made. I was going to give you instructions but I slipped into a coma. The Baking Fairy will not bite you in your sleep if you buy it from a shop.

22 Meringues

Ok, ok, so I know meringues are not British, but they were originally French and parts of France were originally ... well they were.

Utensils
1 medium bowl
1 baking sheet
Greaseproof paper to cover the baking sheet
1 electric mixer

Ingredients
2 egg whites
3½oz/100g caster sugar (ordinary sugar will work but the texture will be slightly coarser)

Method
Pre-heat the oven to 100C/200F/¼ gas mark.
Whisk the egg whites until they form soft peaks (and look like shaving foam).
Whisk in half the sugar.
Fold in the rest of the sugar with a metal spoon.
Put the greaseproof paper on the baking sheet.
Put 8 blobs of the mixture equally on the baking sheet.
Bake for 1½–2 hours or until the meringues are dry and crispy.
When completely cold, sandwich together with whipped cream.
Add some fruit to turn them into health food.

BOVRIL "doffs the cap" to the splendid women of Britain . . .

Women's contributions to the war effort are so vast, so vital, that no words can do justice to them. Whether in uniform or overall, at home or at the work bench, their courage and keenness are outstanding. Bovril salutes the women of Britain.

HOT BOVRIL CHEERS!

23 Osborne Pudding

This is a luxurious version of bread and butter pudding, named after the royal residence on the Isle of Wight. The Victorians had a passion for chilled desserts and ices, and Queen Victoria was no exception; this was one of her favourite dishes.

This dish uses four egg yolks so I would recommend planning to make some meringues or a whipped dessert in order to use up the remaining egg whites.

Utensils

1 small saucepan
1 medium bowl
1 sieve
1 bain-marie or pan of hot water with a bowl on top
1 wooden spoon
1 metal spoon
4 dessert bowls

Ingredients

3 slices of brown bread – crusts cut off
Orange marmalade – fine cut is more delicate
½ pint/1,300ml of milk
3floz/90ml double cream
4 egg yolks
1½oz/145g caster sugar
1 tablespoon sweet sherry
½ pint/300ml whipped cream
Almonds or glacé cherries, angelica or orange jelly slice to decorate

Method

Spread the bread with marmalade and cut into little squares.
Put the milk and double cream into a saucepan and heat until warm.
Whisk the egg yolks and sugar in a bowl and pour it into the
    milk and cream.

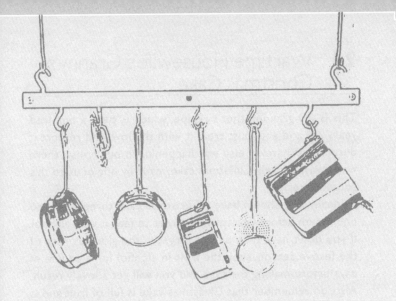

Stir until it is well blended then sieve to get out any stringy bits.

If using a bain-marie, transfer the mixture to that, otherwise return the mixture to the bowl and place it over a pan of hot water.

Heat, stirring continuously until the mixture has thickened into a nice custard.

Allow to cool a little.

Fold in the brown bread, sherry and whipped cream.

Turn into the serving dishes and chill thoroughly.

Decorate attractively with the almonds or whatever you choose, and serve.

24 Wartime Housewife's Granny's Christmas Cake

This is my grandmother's recipe, which is over a hundred years old and you must treat it with the love and respect it deserves. Whatever else was happening in our house, there was always a lovely Christmas cake, made by one of us, to this gorgeous recipe.

Ideally, one should bake a Christmas cake three weeks to one month before Christmas, in order to feed it with alcohol. If you don't have time or just forget in the glorious rush of the festive season, soak the fruit in alcohol for a couple of days before making the cake and you will get a lovely result. Also, do remember that Christmas cake is full of fruit and is therefore health food.

A small Christmas cake makes a lovely and welcome gift, particularly for someone who doesn't have the time to bake, or is perhaps on their own and can't manage a bigger one. Adjust the quantities accordingly.

Utensils

1 large mixing bowl
1 food mixer
Cake tin – appropriate to shape and quantity (this one will fit a 10in/24cm round tin)
Greaseproof paper
Newspaper
String

Ingredients

8oz/240g soft brown sugar

8oz/240g butter

4 eggs – beaten

1½ tablespoons black treacle

9oz/270g wholemeal self-raising flour

1½ teaspoons mixed spice

14oz/420g raisins

14oz/420g sultanas

12oz/360g currants

6oz/180g glacé cherries – halved

2oz/60g chopped almonds

Brandy or rum for feeding – allow a quarter bottle to be on the safe side; after all it's not likely to go to waste!

Method

Cream the butter and sugar until very pale.

Beat in the eggs, then mix in the treacle.

Gradually fold the flour into the mixture.

Once it is all combined, add all the other ingredients.

Spoon the cake mixture into the prepared tin, leaving a deep indentation in the middle so that it rises flat.

Wrap newspaper around the outside of the tin, leaving a good 2in of paper above the top of the tin.

Secure the paper with string (do not use plastic string as this will melt).

Bake at 150C/300F/gas mark 2 for 2 hours, then at 140C/275F/ gas mark 1 for 1 hour.

Remove the newspaper, then leave to cool in the tin.

Each day, drizzle half a capful of brandy or rum over the cake until you are ready to marzipan and ice it.

How to line your cake tin

When baking a heavy fruit cake, you need to line the tin properly with greaseproof paper.

Lay out your greaseproof paper on a flat surface and trace round the bottom of the tin twice.

Cut out the two circles and set aside.

Cut a long strip, the circumference of the tin and about 1in/2½cm deeper than the tin. Make small cuts at regular intervals all along one long edge.

Grease the tin then place circle of greaseproof in the bottom.

Grease this circle of paper lightly then put the long length of paper around the inside of the tin, snipped side at the bottom so that is overlaps the ready greased circle.

Then place the second circle of greaseproof paper on top of that.

25   Bath Buns

I went to Bath recently and sat outside the cathedral with a cup of Earl Grey and a Bath bun. I'd never had one before and it was a thing of beauty. Bath buns date from the mid-1700s although the original 'Bath cakes' were more like dragees with the dough centre covered in caraway seeds and layers of hardened sugar coating. They should not be confused with Sally Lunns which also come from Bath.

You mustn't be frightened of cooking with yeast; if you treat it well it will behave itself and the results will make you as pleased as punch.

Utensils
1 medium mixing bowl
1 large mixing bowl
Cling film
Somewhere warm to let the dough rise
A sifter or sieve
A fine grater for lemon rind
2 baking sheets
1 clean tea towel
1 pastry brush
1 cooling rack

Ingredients
¾oz/20g fresh yeast
¼pint/150ml warm milk
2oz/50g sugar
12oz/350g strong white plain flour
1 egg – beaten
5oz/150g sultanas
2 lemons
2oz/50g butter – softened
A pinch of cinnamon
2oz/60g cube sugar – crushed
1 beaten egg for glazing

Method

Cream the yeast with the milk, one teaspoon of sugar and two tablespoons of flour until it is smooth.

Leave in a warm place for 20 minutes.

Sift the remaining flour into a bowl and make a well in the centre.

Add the remaining sugar and the yeast mixture and mix with enthusiasm.

Add the butter and mix well.

Knead the dough lightly and form into a ball.

Place in a bowl, cover with cling film and leave to rise in a warm place for half an hour.

Sprinkle the dough with the sultanas, cinnamon, lemon rind and half of the sugar.

'Tear' it in until they are evenly distributed throughout the dough.

Switch the oven on to 230C/450F/gas mark 8.

Divide into 16 buns, place on the greased baking sheets, leaving plenty of room for them to grow.

Cover with the tea towel and leave to rise for 20 minutes.

Brush the buns lightly with the beaten egg and then sprinkle on the remaining sugar.

Bake in the pre-heated oven for approx 10–12 minutes until golden on the top.

26 Wartime Housewife's Chocolate and Beetroot Cake

Now calm down, beetroot is lovely and the word 'beet' should give you a clue that this cake is very sweet, quite groovy and almost certainly health food because it has vegetables in it. We're quite at home with carrot cake after all and this cake is moist, delicious and totally luxurious. Also, because of the beetroot, it really lasts. Like it's going to …

Utensils
1 blender
1 large mixing bowl
1 medium bowl
1 electric beater
2 1lb/500g loaf tins – greased and floured
1 wire rack

Ingredients
1 cooked beetroot – about 6–7oz/180–200g
A pinch of salt
8oz/240g plain flour
4oz/120g cocoa powder
1 rounded tablespoon baking powder
9oz/280g demerara sugar
3 large eggs
2 tsp vanilla essence
7floz/200ml vegetable oil
4oz/120g chocolate – chopped

Filling and Icing
8oz/240g cream cheese
2oz/60g mascarpone
6oz/180g icing sugar

Method

Pre-heat the oven to 190C/375F/gas mark 5.

Remove the skin and nobbly bits from the beetroot and chop it into pieces.

Put it in the blender and whizz it up.

Pour into the large bowl and add the salt, flour, cocoa, baking powder, sugar, eggs and vanilla.

Beat like billy-oh until it is thoroughly mixed (you could do the whole lot in the blender if you have a big one).

Now, still beating, steadily add the oil.

Stir in the chocolate.

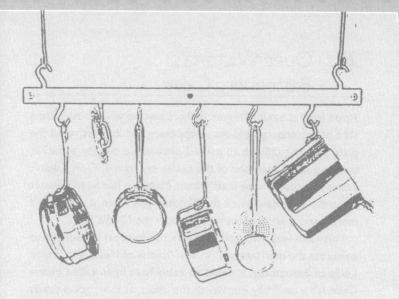

Divide the mixture between the two prepared tins.

Bake for 30–40 minutes or until a skewer or thin knife comes out virtually clean.

If the cakes start to brown too quickly, cover the tins with foil for the rest of the cooking.

Meanwhile, prepare the topping/filling. Beat the cream cheese, mascarpone and icing sugar together in a bowl. And that's it!

When cooked, remove the cakes from the oven and leave to cool on a wire tray.

When completely cold, use half the cream to sandwich the two cakes together and swirl the remaining half nicely on the top.

27 Queen Victoria's Battenberg Cake

Apart from the nut allergists, is there anyone who doesn't like a slice of Battenberg? It looks so appealing and impressive on the plate and isn't difficult to make. I once made one for a market stall and had a member of the public say to me, 'Ooh, I didn't know you could make that!' Mmm. Marzipan has been a sweet favourite in Britain since the Middle Ages when it was called marchpane; it probably came over from the Middle East.

This cake was invented in the Victorian royal household to celebrate the marriage of Princess Victoria of Hesse and Prince Louis of Battenberg. It could so easily have been called Hesse Cake. It's a bit fiddly, but worth the effort, as most good things are. Incidentally, this cake freezes well, so you can make a few and knock them dead at the next fete.

Utensils
1 large mixing bowl
1 medium mixing bowl
1 electric mixer
2 1lb/500g loaf tins
1 wire rack

Ingredients
6oz/180g softened butter
6oz/180g caster sugar
5oz/150g self-raising flour
3 eggs
¼ teaspoon vanilla extract
Pink food colouring
6oz/180g seedless raspberry jam
1lb/500g marzipan
Icing sugar for dusting and rolling out

Method

Pre-heat the oven to 180C/375F/gas mark 4.

Grease and flour the loaf tins.

Put the butter and sugar into the larger bowl and beat until very light.

Gradually add the flour and the baking powder.

Then beat in the eggs and vanilla.

Put half the mixture into the smaller bowl and colour it pink.

Put the yellow mixture into one prepared tin and the pink mixture into the other.

Bake for about 10–15 minutes. Test it with a skewer or thin knife – it should come out clean.

Leave to cool on a wire rack.

When cool, trim the edges to get any brown bits off.

Cut each cake in half lengthways and trim so they are the same length.

Stick the cake bars together with the jam into a block of four to give a chequer-board effect.

Lightly dust the work surface with icing sugar and roll out the marzipan to about ¼in thick.

Brush the outside of the sponges with jam and wrap the marzipan round the cake, leaving the ends showing.

Trim the marzipan to a nice neat oblong shape with the join at the bottom.

Et voila!

28   Blackberry Cordial

I've chosen blackberries for this cordial because they grow freely in the hedgerow. Almost any fruit would work; raspberry would be delicious or blackcurrants for a homemade Ribena. The point is that homemade cordials are utterly delicious and imagine the admiring looks of your friends as you present them with a refreshing fruity drink and, when they ask where you bought it, you say diffidently, 'Oh, I made it myself actually …'

Utensils

1 preserving pan or very large saucepan with a lid
1 potato masher
1 jelly bag *or* a sieve lined with muslin

Ingredients

2lb/1kg blackberries
White sugar
¼pint/150ml water
2 tablespoons lemon juice
1 teaspoon citric or tartaric acid

..*Shoot straight, Lady*

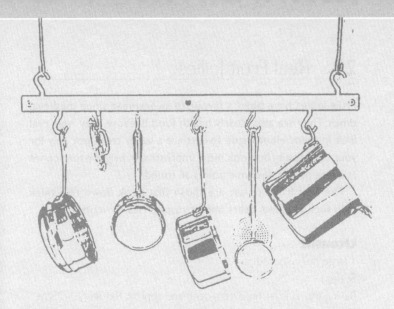

Method

Put the blackberries into the large pan with the water.

Put onto a low heat for about 10 minutes until the juices are obviously present.

Leave to cool for 10 minutes.

Crush the fruit with a potato masher or similar.

Sieve into a large clean bowl and squeeze every drop of juice out of the fruit pulp.

Measure the juice and add an equal quantity of sugar e.g. 600ml juice to 600g sugar (1 pint juice to 20oz sugar).

Add the lemon juice.

Return the liquid to the pan and heat gently until the sugar has completely dissolved.

Bring to the boil for about a minute.

Skim off any scum and add the citric or tartaric acid and stir it in well.

Pour immediately into sterilized bottles, label and store.

29   Real Fruit Jellies

Fruit jellies have been a favourite sweetmeat since medieval times. They are also clearly health food because they have real fruit in them. Homemade sweets are a super treat, not only for your own family, but look most impressive in bright paper cones at a fete or sale. Brownie points all round.

The best fruits to use are those that cook down to a thick pulp such as plums, pears, apples, raspberries, apricots etc.

Utensils
1 large heavy based pan
Scales
Baking tray at least 1in/2½cm deep and approx. 8x10in /20x25cm
Greaseproof paper
Petit four cases

Ingredients
2lb/900g fruit
1 lemon – squeezed
White sugar
Fruit flavouring if required
Caster sugar for coating

Method
Line the baking tin with greaseproof paper.
Peel, chop, skin, stone, core etc. the fruit as necessary.
Place it in the pan with just enough water to keep it moving
    while it's cooking
Bring it to the boil, stirring continuously.
Reduce the heat and simmer gently for about an hour or until
    the fruit is completely soft.
Sieve the fruit to rid it of any pips, bits of skin etc.
Now weigh the puree and add an equal quantity of sugar.

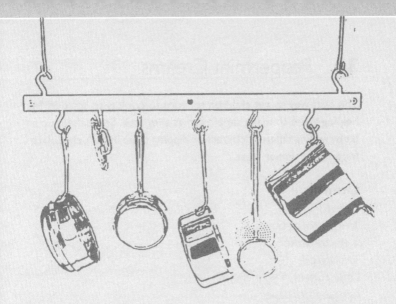

Stir in the lemon juice.

Return the puree to the pan and set it on a low heat, stirring continuously until the sugar is dissolved.

Turn up the heat and boil quickly until a thick paste is formed and the mixture is about to set.

Add any flavourings you wish to now.

Pour the mixture into the lined baking tin and leave to go completely cold.

Cut into squares or shapes and roll in the caster sugar.

Place each one in a petit four case and store in an airtight tin.

30   Peppermint Creams

The best way to get children to learn to cook is to start off by helping them to make simple things they love. Snazz them up a bit by adding different colours or dipping them in dark chocolate for an after dinner treat.

Utensils
1 sieve
1 large mixing bowl
1 electric mixer
1 rolling pin
Little cutters of your choice
Greaseproof paper
A tray of some sort

Ingredients
1lb/450g icing sugar
4 tablespoons condensed milk
A few drops of peppermint extract

Method
Sift the icing sugar into a mixing bowl.
Add the condensed milk and mix together well until smooth and creamy.
Add the peppermint extract* a little at a time to get the strength you like, working it well with your hands so that the flavouring is evenly distributed throughout the 'dough'.
Dust your work surface with icing sugar.
Roll out the mixture to about ¼in/½ cm thick and cut into nice shapes.
Place a bit of greaseproof on the tray and put the peppermint creams on it, leaving them to set in a cool place.

* If adding colourings, now's the time to do it

4

HOUSEHOLD TIPS

CLEANING

- Don't buy separate cleaning fluids for every different job. It's a con. A decent, all-purpose **household cleaner** will manage most things as will an own brand bleach and a packet of soda crystals. Better still, invest in some eco cloths. My sister bought me some four years ago and they're still doing the job.
- Putting lemon juice in the cleaning water will **disinfect work surfaces** as well as anything else.
- Essential oil on a damp cloth, wiped over your radiators will **fragrance** your house as well as any air freshener, costs much less and can be tailored to your own taste.
- Remove **lipstick** from fabric by spraying the mark with hairspray, leave for five minutes, wipe and then wash as usual.
- To get a **white cup ring** out of a leather topped table, apply some matching shoe polish to the leather, working it in well with a toothbrush then buff it off with a soft cloth. Repeat if necessary.

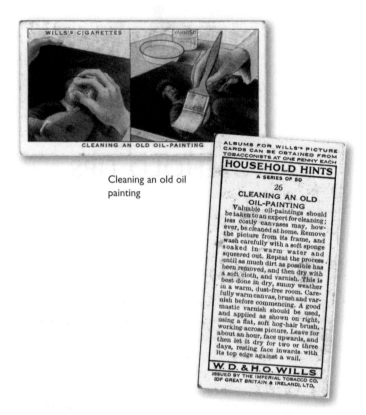

Cleaning an old oil painting

- To remove **limescale** from a showerhead, cover the head with a plastic bag filled with 2oz/50g of bicarbonate of soda and 7floz/200ml vinegar. Fasten the bag loosely and leave for an hour. Rinse.
- When cleaning decorative panels or carving on **furniture**, use a soft toothbrush to get the dust out of the detailing.
- When **washing floor**s, walls and paintwork, use two buckets – one with your cleaning solution and one for rinsing.
- **White enamel sinks** are easily stained and scratched. A gentle and very effective way of cleaning a sink and keeping it white is to put the plug in, pour in one

cupful of biological washing powder, then fill the sink with hot water. Stir it round well to dissolve the powder and leave it for an hour or longer if you can. Rinse well with cold water.

- To remove **crayon marks** from walls, dab a little lighter fluid on a clean cloth and wipe at the mark until it disappears.
- **Soda crystals** are great because they are very cheap, have many uses and they break down harmlessly in the soil. General cleaning: dissolve a handful of soda crystals in a bucket of hot water. Clean things.
- Always wash **silver cutlery** as soon as possible after use to prevent it tarnishing.
- To clean a lot of **silver cutlery** quickly, put some aluminium foil in a plastic bowl and place the cutlery on top. Pour in enough boiling water to cover it then add 2oz/60g of baking soda. Leave it for 10 or 15 minutes and then rinse and dry. The foil and baking soda method can also be used on silver jewellery.
- To remove **white marks** from wood, put a tablespoon of cigarette ash in a small dish or saucer and mix it with water, drop by drop, until it forms a thick paste. Using a soft cloth rub the paste gently, but resolutely, into the white area. Let it soak in for a few minutes then wipe off. Treat again as necessary until the ring has gone.
- Use household soap to scrub **stone floors**. Not only does it lift dirt that modern cleaning solutions simply won't, it builds up a very thin protective layer which discourages dirt from sinking in. Use two buckets as above and a mop to rinse the soap off. Scrub stone or slate floors on your hands and knees with a brush. It's far more effective and has the added benefit of burning off those calories.
- Clean **windows** with scrunched up dampened newspaper.

- To get **hair and lint** off clothes or fabric apply strips of parcel tape or sellotape then peel them off.
- **Clean artificial plants** and flowers with a hairdryer set high and cool before you dust and vacuum.
- Sweep the stairs with a paintbrush – a medium sized paintbrush will get into the corners and between the rails more easily than even the vacuum.
- Take advantage of a snowfall to **clean your rugs**. Place the rugs face down on the snow and put some clean snow on the upper side, and beat the rugs. A lot of dirt will fall through.

Cleaning a thermos flask

WILL'S CIGARETTES

CLEANING A THERMOS FLASK

ALBUMS FOR WILL'S'S PICTURE
CARDS CAN BE OBTAINED FROM
TOBACCONISTS AT ONE PENNY EACH

HOUSEHOLD HINTS
A SERIES OF 50

43

CLEANING A THERMOS FLASK

Beverages carried in a thermos flask cannot be enjoyed to the full unless the flask is kept scrupulously clean. To cleanse a stained flask, crush some eggshells and drop them into the flask. Add a little vinegar and shake vigorously; then half-fill with water and allow flask to stand for some time. The flask should be shaken again before being emptied, and thoroughly rinsed. When standing it upside-down to dry, there is less risk of the flask being knocked over if it is stood inside a jug. Thermos flasks, when empty, should always be left uncorked, as this prevents them becoming musty.

W. D. & H. O. WILLS
ISSUED BY THE IMPERIAL TOBACCO CO.
(OF GREAT BRITAIN & IRELAND), LTD.

- **Chewing gum** can be removed from fabric by freezing. If it's on the carpet put a bag full of ice cubes on it and when it's frozen gently pick it off. If you get chewing gum on clothes, put the garment in the freezer until the gum goes solid then bend the fabric to make it crack, then pick it off.

- Get rid of the **smell of wee** on mattresses by dampening the stain with a cloth and rubbing in some borax. Let it dry then vacuum up.

- To **stop shoes being smelly**, pour some bicarbonate of soda into the shoes and leave overnight. Obviously, shake out the soda before wearing them.

- To remove **greasy marks** from tables, rub them with lemon juice until the mark has gone.

- To polish your **car windscreen**, make a thin paste with water and baking powder and rub it all over the screen. Rinse it well with water and polish off with a soft, lint-free cloth.

- To clean **leather furniture** and suitcases, wash with suds made of household soap and a little warm water. Rinse off with cold water, dry it, then gloss it with a little egg white. Allow to dry slightly then polish with a soft duster Alternatively, leather furniture and shoes can be cleaned using the inside of a banana skin. Rub the skin all over and then buff up with a soft cloth. Astonishingly, this also works on silver.

- To **renovate leather** furniture – wash it with a little soapy water. When it is dry gently rub in some Vaseline with your hands. Leave it over night then polish up with a soft cloth.

- Use baby wipes to clean your **computer** keyboard.

- To get rid of **tea stains** from mugs and teapots, make a strong solution of bicarbonate of soda and water and leave for an hour. Rinse well and store upside down with the lid off.

- To clean a **Panama hat**, melt a little household soap and a little ammonia in water and sponge off the marks. Rinse with water to which a little glycerine has been added and that will keep it supple.
- To clean **straw hats**, put a teaspoon of flowers of sulphur into a saucer and squeeze the juice of a lemon over it. Apply this mixture to the hat with a nailbrush then rinse in cold water.
- Keep **old toothbrushes** in your cleaning box as they are ideal for getting into nooks such as round the bottom of taps, sink plugs and the fittings on the lavatory. When

Three uses for old newspapers

polishing fretwork on brass or silver, wrap the toothbrush in a soft cloth.

- Newspaper contains a weak acid and is a super way to **polish glass**. Wash your glass with water, then scrunch up some newspaper to dry and polish it.

- To clean the glass on the doors of a **woodburning stove**, apply a strong cleaning fluid, such as a shop's own brand general cleaner, with a plastic scourer and rub hard until the greasy brown marks have come off. Dry and polish using scrunched up newspaper. If you do this frequently, it will only take a few minutes each week to keep them gleaming and your lovely fire visible.

- If you spill **wax onto fabric**, treat the area with a little white spirit, then sponge the wax off with a clean cloth. Do a test first on an inconspicuous area of the fabric or carpet to ensure that it is colourfast.

- To remove **hot wax** on a wooden floor, gently scrape the wax off with a pallet knife or ice scraper. If the wax has left white spots on the wood, mix up some cigarette ash with a little water to make a thick paste. Rub this into the wood in small circular movements. Wipe off and polish. Repeat until the white mark has gone.

- Deodorise your **dishwasher** by placing a generous handful of bicarbonate of soda on the bottom. It will rinse away when you do your next load.

- The quickest way to get small **blood stains** out of fabric is to spit on it as much as you can. The enzymes in your mouth dissolve the stain.

- To prevent **flies** from marking windows, mirrors and pictures, clean with a tiny bit of Brasso – it gives a brilliant polish and saves much work when flies are about.

- If your **microwave** gets a bit whiffy, even though you've cleaned it, rub half a lemon all over the inside, then wipe it clean.

- Clean the glass front of your **cooker** with a thick paste of wood ash and a little water. Apply with a damp sponge then rinse off with water and wipe dry.
- To clean plush **upholstered chairs**, apply a little household soap with a damp sponge and gently rub well into the material. Rinse with clean water – it brings up the colour wonderfully.
- To **clean raincoats** – shred 2oz/60g of household soap and dissolve it in four pints of boiling water. Apply to the soiled and greasy marks on the raincoat and then wash clean with a piece of flannel. Dry and press.
- Remove mud or grease from **suede shoes** by rubbing them gently but firmly with sandpaper.
- To make **children's painting** accidents easier to clean, mix the paint with a little washing up liquid and it will come off easily.
- To remove **ink stains** from fabric rub with a ripe tomato then wash in lukewarm water.
- **Coffee stains** can be cleaned with pure glycerine. Rub it well into the stain then leave for half an hour. Wash it out with a little household soap.
- Protect your **dishwasher** by wiping the plates with newspaper before putting them in. This helps prevent those annoying sludge deposits.
- If your **lavatory** is really badly stained, push the water out by pumping the loo brush up and down then get the last of the water out using a loo brush with a cloth wrapped round it. Then put your loo cleaner down so that it is not diluted and leave it for five or ten minutes before giving it a good scrub and then flush.
- Clean **pewter** by rubbing it all over with cabbage leaves.
- Keep **drains in sinks** clear by putting a big handful of soda crystals down, leave it for half an hour then rinse through with boiling water.

Removing seawater
stains from brown shoes

- To remove **sea water** stains from shoes, dissolve a teaspoon of soda crystals in an egg cup of hot milk. Leave to cool then apply the warm mixture to the stains and rub in well. When dry, polish as usual.
- To avoid dirtying woodwork when **polishing brass** fittings, make a shield of stiff cardboard by cutting out the shape of the fitting. Keep it to hand and it will last for years.
- Cleaning your **mincing machine** – it can be the very devil getting bits of fat out and to dry it after washing. Put pieces of stale bread through and it will take the fat and damp with it.
- Remove **liquid stains on brass** by rubbing with lemon juice.

- To prevent **mildew** in your bathroom, clean the tiles and around the shower wall thoroughly and apply a layer of car wax. Buff it with a soft cloth.
- To **bleach clothes** naturally, dip them in water and then spread them on green grass to dry.
- To get **biro marks** out of fabric, apply methylated spirit with cotton wool or a white piece of towelling.
- A non-chemical way to **clean carpets** quickly and cheaply is to sprinkle them with hot bran and then vacuum it up on full power.
- To **wash antique lace**, make some soap jelly by mixing household soap with boiling water. Put the jelly in a jam

Some uses for salt

ALBUMS FOR WILLS'S PICTURE CARDS CAN BE OBTAINED FROM TOBACCONISTS AT ONE PENNY EACH

HOUSEHOLD HINTS

A SERIES OF 50

40

SOME USES OF SALT

Every housewife should keep a good store of salt, which is not only indispensable in cooking, but has many general uses. Here are three: A. Should eggs be accidentally cracked before or while being boiled, add a teaspoonful of salt to the water. This will prevent the white (albumen) of the egg boiling out. B. To keep cut flowers fresh, a little salt should be added to the water. C. Egg-spoons soon tarnish in use. The unsightly stains may be removed by rubbing briskly with a little salt on a damp cloth.

W. D. & H. O. WILLS

ISSUED BY THE IMPERIAL TOBACCO CO. (OF GREAT BRITAIN & IRELAND), LTD.

jar with a lid and put the lace in with it. Put the jar in a pan of hot water and simmer for 2–3 hours. Rinse.

- To keep **brick floors** a nice rich colour, add a little paraffin to the bucket when you wash the floor.

- To clean water bottles or **decanters**, tear up small pieces of newspaper, put them in the bottles then fill up with water. Leave for 5 minutes then give them a good shake. The stains will vanish and glass will be bright.

- To stop your **cooker top** becoming caked with grease, sprinkle a little salt over the hob top before frying and the grease won't stick.

- To remove **mildew** from hard surfaces, apply hydrogen peroxide 3% directly to the area then wipe clean.

- To clean **copper**, apply a thin layer of ketchup with a cloth and leave it for 10–30 minutes. Rinse with clean water and dry immediately.

DIY

- Keep tiny jam jars or condiment jars to store **nails and screws** in.

- When storing **paint**, put a layer of cling film over the tin before you put the lid on to keep it fresh.

- If you're filling **cracks in woodwork** before painting, mix a little of the paint with some flour and fill the crack. When you paint, the filler will be much less noticeable.

- If you have lost the integral **plug** for your washbasin, replace it with a large glass marble.

- To remove **paint smears** or splashes from window panes, rub lightly with a piece of eraser and it will remove the paint without scratching.

- Reduce **paint smells** by leaving half an onion on a plate in the room you have painted.

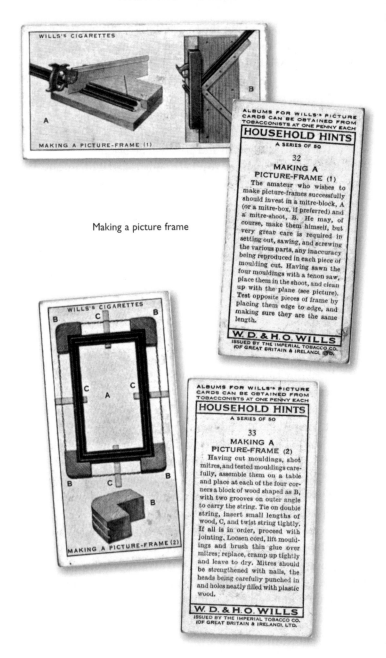

Making a picture frame

- To take small dents out of **wood**, put a wet cloth over the dent then place a hot iron on the cloth. Repeat until the dent disappears.
- To ease **sticking drawers** – rub a little household soap along the upper edges of the drawer. The smell will also deter moths.
- To **tighten scissors**, place a red hot poker on each side of the rivet.
- Extend the reach of your **vacuum cleaner** by putting the inside of a kitchen roll or foil roll onto the end of the nozzle.
- Rub some chalk on the tip of a **screwdriver** to prevent it slipping.
- If you suspect your **lavatory cistern** is leaking, pour a teaspoon of food colouring into it. If it is leaking, the coloured water will appear in the bowl. If so, you should contact your plumber.
- When you are **painting a ceiling**, help prevent splatters and sticky handles by pushing the handle through a large paper plate.
- To **drive a nail** firmly into a soft or flaky wall, open up the hole and fill it with a little plaster of Paris mixed with water. Put the nail in and leave to dry. You could also use ordinary filler but plaster sets more quickly.
- If you can't **hammer** anything without hammering your-self, push the nail through a piece of cardboard and hold the edge of the cardboard while you hammer the nail in.
- To **patch wallpaper** to hide a tear or stain, tear the paper to fit the shape instead of cutting it – it will be far less noticeable.
- If the knob comes off a **saucepan lid**, replace it with a cork. Put a screw in from underneath and screw the cork firmly on top. This will also be heat resistant.
- **Emergency filler** (such as when some evil landlord is coming to inspect and you can't get to the shops). Mix

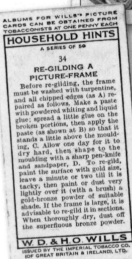

Re-gilding a picture frame

some sawdust with a little glue to form a stiff paste. Press it into the holes and it will set hard.

- To make a **cork mat** to protect your kitchen worktops, save all your corks and push them through a piece of wire netting. Trim the corks so that the mat is even.
- Fishing line is great for **hanging pictures** – it's strong and almost invisible.
- **Gilt picture frames** which are past their best can be renovated by washing them in water in which onions have been boiled.

- If you're worried about something **leaking from your car**, put a large sheet of cardboard under the car overnight. The position and the colour of the drip will help your mechanic to identify the problem.
- To **loosen a tight screw** from wood, place a screwdriver in the top of it and give it a sharp tap with a hammer. This should loosen it.
- If a knob comes off a **kitchen drawer** or cupboard, a temporary replacement can be made using an empty cotton reel.

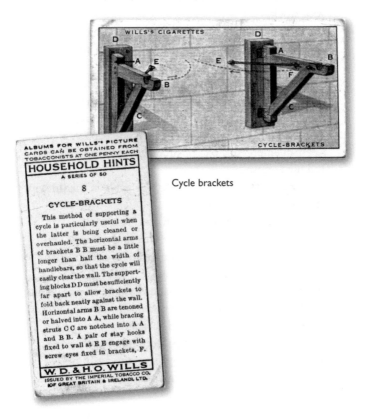

Cycle brackets

ALBUMS FOR WILLS'S PICTURE CARDS CAN BE OBTAINED FROM TOBACCONISTS AT ONE PENNY EACH

HOUSEHOLD HINTS

A SERIES OF 50

8

CYCLE-BRACKETS

This method of supporting a cycle is particularly useful when the latter is being cleaned or overhauled. The horizontal arms of brackets B B must be a little longer than half the width of handlebars, so that the cycle will easily clear the wall. The supporting blocks D D must be sufficiently far apart to allow brackets to fold back neatly against the wall. Horizontal arms B B are tenoned or halved into A A, while bracing struts C C are notched into A A and B B. A pair of stay hooks fixed to wall at E E engage with screw eyes fixed in brackets, F.

W. D. & H. O. WILLS

ISSUED BY THE IMPERIAL TOBACCO CO. (OF GREAT BRITAIN & IRELAND), LTD.

- There is no point in **washing ceilings**. It is far quicker to get rid of any dust or cobwebs and slap another coat of paint on them.
- If a **ceiling is really greasy** or brown from smokers, it should be cleaned with sugar soap.

FOOD

- Use dental floss to lift **biscuits** off a baking tray.
- Before throwing away **Marmite** jars, swoosh them round with a bit of boiling water and save the liquid to add to your stock.
- Don't waste money on expensive food clips, use plastic **clothes pegs** to seal bags. This way you can colour-code the contents as well.
- If you have a **glut of garlic**, keep it fresh by peeling it and putting the cloves into a jar of olive oil. You can also use the oil as an extra flavour in cooking or salad dressings.
- You can use the above tip with onions and peppers as well.
- Keep an emergency bag of **sliced onions** in the freezer and use as fresh.
- Keep **cakes fresh** by putting half an apple in the tin with the cake to keep it moist.
- When **stuffing poultry**, put the stuffing into a cheesecloth bag and then shove that in the cavity. The juices and flavours will still mingle but the stuffing can be pulled out in one go with no waste.
- **Plan as many meals** as you can in advance so that you can get the food you need, thereby potentially reducing waste.
- **Cook from scratch** to avoid packaging.
- Use an old tuna can as an **egg poacher** by removing both ends of the can and popping it into a pan of simmering water. Drop the egg into the middle.

- Take **tupperware boxes** to the meat, fish and deli counters in the supermarket and ask them to put your food in those with the bar code stuck to the lid. Some will refuse, but most won't and if they do – make a fuss! Independent shops are much more amenable to this idea.
- **Sugar bags and flour bags** are ideal for re-use as they are lightly waxed on the outside to keep the original contents dry. Use them to wrap sandwiches and cake for packed lunches.
- To **peel hot beetroots** plunge them straight into cold water; the skin will peel off like a glove.

A handwritten account book from 1911 for Chitty, Hodges & Higgs, butchers and farmers from Walton-on-Thames, Surrey

- To stop **fried eggs** from breaking or sticking add a teaspoon of flour to the cooking fat.
- To refresh **frozen fish**, defrost it in milk. You can then use the milk to make a lovely sauce afterwards.
- If you run out of **butter** and you can't get any more quickly, beat a little milk into what you already have and it will stretch further.
- Use a funnel to **separate eggs**.
- To roll a **Swiss roll** quickly and easily, turn it out onto a damp cloth and just pull up evenly on the end of the cloth as if tipping the sponge off it.
- **Coffee filters** make useful splash covers for your microwave.
- Freeze **leftover wine** into ice cube trays for use in sauces and stocks.
- When **boiling milk**, put a large glass marble into the saucepan. The marble automatically stirs the milk and prevents the pan from burning.
- **Store berries and fruit** in a colander in the fridge to stop them going off so quickly.
- Keep **mould off cheese** by putting a cube of sugar inside the wrapping.
- If **peanut butter** gets a bit dry, mix in a spoonful of runny honey – mix it well.
- **Nicely sealed fruit pies** – to prevent fruit boiling up and spoiling the look of pies and tarts, seal the edges with milk instead of water.
- To remove the **smell of onions** from your hands after chopping, rub them with a bit of celery.
- To remove the **smell of fish** from your hands, rub them with lemon juice or salt.
- To **pick fruit** that is high on the tree safely, take an 8oz/240g coffee tin and sharpen one edge on the inner rim. Put some cloth or kitchen roll into the bottom. Attach the tin to a long stick then when this is put under the fruit it will drop safely into the tin.

- Always add a little oil to butter if you're **frying** to stop the butter turning brown.
- Test **eggs for freshness** by putting them one at a time into a jug of water. If it sinks to the bottom it's fresh, if it floats it's stale. If one end lifts up slightly, I'd risk it if I were you.
- **Cutting fresh bread** – dip your bread knife into hot water before cutting and you'll be able to get quite thin slices without the whole thing tearing and crumbling.
- Save energy **boiling eggs** by placing the eggs into a pan of boiling water, remove from the heat, put the lid on and leave for 5 or 6 minutes depending on whether they have come from the fridge or are at room temperature.
- To keep **fresh herbs** and leaves fresh for longer, roll them up in a wet cloth.
- Wear swimming goggles when **chopping onions** to stop you crying.
- Revive **rancid butter** by cutting it up into small pieces and putting them into a bowl of milk for an hour. Drain off the milk, rinse in salt water and form back into a pat.
- If you **burn milk in a pan**, remove the burnt taste by putting a jug of the milk into a pan of cold water, adding a pinch of salt and stirring well.
- **Ripen tomatoes** quickly by putting them in a drawer out of direct sunlight.
- Never put **tomatoes** in the fridge as they lose their taste.
- **Ripen avocados** quickly by putting them in a bag with a banana or putting them in a warm place like the airing cupboard or near the woodburner.
- **Egg whites** will whip up much more quickly if you add a tiny pinch of fine salt.
- To prevent **table salt** from clagging up, put a few grains of rice or a dried bean or two in the salt cellar.

- To **stop milk from boiling over**, rub a little butter round the rim of the pan. Alternatively a metal funnel in the pan will perform the same function.
- To stop **potatoes from sprouting**, put a couple of apples in with them.
- **Make stock** from meat or chicken bones by putting them in the slow cooker with some water and stock vegetables. You won't burn your pan and the house won't smell as much.
- When **plucking a fowl**, pour boiling water over them first – the feathers come off much more quickly and won't fly about as much.

Sewing, Knitting and Mending

- **Mend** your children's clothes and darn your socks. Just because you can buy a new pair of trousers in Primark for £2 doesn't mean you should. You can do mending while watching TV or listening to the radio.
- To stop **sewing thread** tangling, thread your needle and then run the needle and thread through a fabric softener sheet to give it a non-stick coating.
- When **knitting socks**, knit mercerised silk or thread in with the wool around the heels and toes to strengthen them.
- To extend the life of **new socks**, make running stitches across each heel out of wool or silk.
- To **thread a needle** with wool more easily, pass the two ends of a short piece of cotton thread through the eye of the needle, then put the end of the wool through the cotton hook. Pull the thread through the eye and the wool will come with it.
- Always do your **mending** before putting clothes in the washing machine as the agitation of the drum will make things worse and loose buttons can damage the machine.

- Use a **stub of candle** as a pincushion – it will also help needles glide more easily and deter rust.

- Keep **odd buttons** together by threading them onto a large safety pin.

- If the **wire** keeps coming out of your **bra or corset**, give up sewing it back in. Pull it out a couple of inches, smear the end with superglue and quickly push it back in. Press firmly to seal it in.

- Make **wire coat hangers** non-slip by wrapping a rubber band round each end.

- Get rid of **iron scorches** by laying the fabric over a large plate on which you have made a jelly of soap, starch and water. Lay a piece of glass over the fabric and leave it in the sun. Keep it damp until all the stain has gone.

- To replace the **tips on shoe laces**, dip the end in melted sealing wax and shape it to a point with your fingers.

- If a **hat band** gets wet and crinkly, iron it by heating a teaspoon and pressing it onto the ribbon.

GENERAL USEFULNESS

- Deodorise a **cat litter tray** cheaply by sprinkling bicarbonate of soda underneath cheap litter or mix it in with the fresh litter.

- Make **cut flowers** last longer by putting them in warm water to which a teaspoon of salt or an aspirin has been added.

- If you need to cook something in a **large pan**, such as a paella, put a metal baking tray over the gas burner and it will heat evenly. You can also use this method to heat two pans on one ring.

- If you have to **transport a picture**, put some masking tape across the glass across and lengthways to stop it splintering if it's damaged.

- If the base plate of your **iron** becomes marked or sticky, clean it with toothpaste and a little wire wool.

- To **dry wet boots** without shrinking and cracking, fill them with oats. These absorb the moisture and swell so the boots hold their shape. The oats can be used again when they have dried so keep them in an airtight jar.
- To **loosen glass stoppers** and rusty screws, apply a little vinegar and then turn sharply – it should loosen almost immediately.
- To **prevent a candle from dripping**, put a little salt around the top of the candle before lighting it.
- To **deter mice** from drawers and cupboards, sprinkle a few drops of peppermint oil into the corners and push cork into any visible holes. Mice can't chew through cork and they hate peppermints. They like Werther's Originals though, so don't mix them up.

Removing stubborn or rusted screws

- In case of a **power cut**, always keep a box of candles and matches in the same place so you know where to find them. Also keep a portable camping stove and spare gas canisters.
- In case of a **power cut**, switch off all electrical appliances and lights as when the electricity returns a power surge could blow a fuse.
- **Sharpening scissors** – use them on the neck of a glass bottle as if you were trying to cut the neck off. Keep doing this until they are sharp.
- To **remove soot** from chimneys without the need for Mr Sweep, make a big, bright fire and put 1oz/30g of flowers of sulphur on it which will clean the flue. Flowers of sulphur are yellow flakes of sulphur (also known as brimstone) which have been used in traditional and complementary therapies for donkey's years. It also has use in the garden and in the preservation of dried fruit.
- Regularly burning potato peelings on the fire will help to prevent **sooty build up** in your chimney.
- If you need to take your **rings** off when cooking or cleaning, pin them to your top using a large safety pin.
- To put out a **small chimney fire**, put wet newspapers on it and the steam will put out the fire.
- **To oil a stiff lock**, apply some oil to the key, insert it into the lock and turn it backwards and forwards a few times.
- Sprinkle some baby powder between your **sheets on hot nights** to keep you feeling cool and smooth.
- Make the most of **heat from radiators** by putting tin foil behind them to deflect heat out into the room instead of being absorbed into the walls.
- To **channel heat from radiators** still further, put a shelf above the radiator to channel the heat flow into the room.

- To make a candle fit the **candlestick**, dip the end in hot water. This will soften it enough to mould to the size you need (within reason).
- If a **candle is too loose** for a holder, either drip a little wax into the holder then push the candle in firmly or wrap a thin strip of gaffer tape or a strip of plaster round the bottom of the candle.
- If you're having a **party for children** or teenagers, cover all your furniture in cling film to protect it.
- To **deter burglars**, put some table lamps on timers in your home so it always looks as though someone is in. I do the same with the kitchen radio.
- To **prevent fabric wrinkling** when you iron it, place a wad of newspaper underneath it.

Repairing cracks in cemented walls

- To **get rid of ants** sprinkle some borax onto their nest or where they are congregating.

- To stop a carpet edge or **rug from curling**, make up a thick starch paste and spread it along the underneath edge. Put some brown paper over the starched edges and iron dry.

- To make the feet of **tights and stockings** last longer, rub the heels and toes with a piece of beeswax.

- A **broken clock** can be a useful aid for taking medicines. Set the hands for when the tablets or medicine next need to be taken.

- Use leftover water from kettles and hot water bottles to **water plants**.

- To **separate glasses** that have stuck together, put cold water into the inner glass and stand the outer one in warm water and they will be easily separated.

- Before doing **muddy gardening**, scrape your fingernails across a bar of soap. When you come to wash your hands, the dirt will wash away without staining.

- To keep **windows from frosting** up or getting condensation, rub them with a little glycerine on a dry cloth.

- To stop an old-fashioned **alarm clock** from ringing too loudly, put a rubber band around the bells.

- If you make a **horrid smell** in the bathroom, light a match and let it burn down – it will burn away the smell.

- If something unpleasant has **blocked your lavatory**, wait until the water in the pan has returned to its normal level and then hurl a bucket of very hot water, with a bit of washing up liquid in it, down it in one go.

- Keep spare room **beds aired** by regularly placing a hot water bottle in the bed. Put the bottle in a different place each week and the bed linen will not get damp or musty.

- To stop the irritation of **insect bites**, dip some soap in cold water and rub it onto the bite.

- **Line drawers and cupboards** with newspaper. If anything gets spilled you can just take the paper out and

Securing a loose knife

replace it with fresh sheets. It also stops the build up of grease and rust marks.

- **Line drawers** in your bedroom with off-cuts of wallpaper and sprinkle a little of your favourite essential oil onto it for cheap and attractive drawer liners.

- If your **door hinges squeak** and you have no oil, a little washing up liquid will do the trick.

- To re-fluff furniture **pressure marks on carpets**, pop an ice cube onto the flattened bit and leave it to melt. When it has dried, vacuum as usual.

- Protect your **computer's** innards by taping a piece of net curtain or old tights (hose) over the air vent to prevent dust getting into the workings and shorting it out.

- Remove scratches from **acrylic baths** with metal polish.
- Keep **silver tea or coffee pots** fresh between uses by popping a couple of sugar lumps inside. Always store with the lids off or open.
- In cold weather, put a handful of salt down the drains last thing at night and put the plug in, to **stop pipes from freezing**.
- **Double glaze your windows** in winter with cling film and sellotape. Run a hair dryer over the surface to tighten up the cling film and make it all but invisible.
- Old carpets can also be cut up and edged to make personalised **car mats.**
- If your **car door lock is frozen**, hold the key over a match or lighter until it is hot, then insert it into the lock. Leave it for a few minutes then try again.
- Make a **string dispenser** out of an empty golden syrup tin. Using a bradawl, make a hole in the centre of the lid, then use a slightly larger Phillips screwdriver to widen the hole. Turn the lid over and place the hole on something hard and just flatten any sharp bits with a hammer. Thread your string through the hole – it keeps string neat and tidy and looks great.
- Always have a couple of cotton **shopping bags** in your handbag or car.
- If you need to use carrier bags, keep them for use as **bin liners**.
- Keep some of your interesting rubbish for **junk modelling** as an activity for the children.
- Keep some jam jars and small bottles with screw lids. Next year they will be there when you have a go at **jam, jellies and syrups**!
- **Wash foil** and use it again.
- Use the **milkman** if you can afford to. If not, plastic milk cartons, cut in half, make very effective **cloches** for seedlings. You can adjust air flow through the lid.

- If clothes are beyond the pale, cut them up for **dusters and cleaning cloths**. Old pants make super dusters.
- Extend the life of **rubber gloves** by pushing a small cotton wool ball into the finger ends.
- If you need odd bits of furniture for general use, see if your **local tip** has a shop and look their first. You'll be amazed at what you can find.
- **Auctions** – the ultimate in re-use from expensive antiques to general housewares. And it's great fun. Have a go at eBay, Freecycle or other similar sites – you'd be amazed what people buy and sell or even give away.
- Use **charity shops** – again you'll be amazed and the benefits are twofold; less waste plus a charity donation.
- **Weather-proof labels** on parcels and letters by rubbing a white candle over the writing.
- Arachnophobes: **spiders absolutely hate conkers**, so place them round your house in the corners where spiders are like to come creeping in. With their dripping fangs, their red glowing eyes and that horrid way they have of appearing to be all hesitant when actually they want to leap into your hair and …
- **Deter ticks** from attaching themselves to you by rubbing Vicks Vapour Rub (or similar) on your legs before you go into the woods or on rough ground.
- Large and **expensive candles** often burn away in the middle and the outside wax either collapses in on itself or you have to trim the outside away, spoiling the candle. When the candle burns down, say, half an inch, take the metal cup off a tea light and place the tea light in the hole. When this burns down, replace it with another tea light. This way the candle always looks lovely and new. Avoid grease build-ups and flare-ups on your grill by placing a piece of bread in the drip pan.
- If you find a trustworthy **car mechanic**, plumber or handyman, stick to them like glue. Move near to where they live, marry them if you have to.

- Use the inner tubes of **loo rolls** and kitchen rolls to keep electrical cables tidy.
- **Make candles last** longer by putting them in the freezer for a couple of hours before burning.
- Use gaffer tape to make temporary repairs to a **tent**.
- Make a quick **draught excluder** by filling old jacket sleeves with rags or the inside of defunct pillows and stitch up the ends. Conversely, to keep heat out, open the windows a little bit and close the curtains.
- Attach a **bell to the back door** so you know if a child has opened it.
- Rub **shoe laces** over a block of soap or beeswax before lacing them as this will make the knots last longer.
- If the plastic ends come off shoe laces, wrap a bit of parcel tape or gaffer tape round the end.
- If you have a **splinter**, soak the skin in oil to soften it and then hold an ice cube against the skin to numb it before removing the splinter.
- If you **car is stuck in the snow**, take the mats out of the car and place them under the rear wheels to give them a bit of grip.

PASTIMES AND AMUSEMENTS

Some of the best games are made up when one is bored or when there seems to be nothing to do. But if you always have a bag full of sewing scraps, paper, paints, glue, packaging and a big dollop of imagination, you need never have another dull moment.

GAMES TO PLAY

Noah's Ark
Each competitor is given the name of an animal, bird, fish or insect and is allowed ten seconds to match it with a song, quotation or poem in which that particular creature appears. For example, if you are given 'horse' you might come up with The Osmonds' song 'Crazy Horses', or the Shakespeare quote 'A horse, a horse, my kingdom for a horse' etc. Then when you run out of animals you could take another subject such as names or emotions.

Murder in the Dark
First of all, cut up some pieces of paper, one for each player. On one piece write 'Murderer' and on another piece, write

'Detective' – leave the rest of the pieces blank. Fold up the papers and allow the players to take a piece out of a hat, but they must not reveal what they have drawn.

The lights are extinguished and the players scatter through the dark rooms. The murderer prowls through the house looking for his victim then suddenly he throws his arms around one of the players who is obliged to let out a blood-curdling scream as he falls dead to the floor. As soon as they hear the scream, all the players must stand exactly where they are and wait. The detective then counts to thirty and then switches the lights on, giving the murderer time to merge with the rest of the players.

Now the investigation begins. The detective makes a note of the position of the victim and the rest of the players. Then he takes everyone out of the room and begins to ask questions. Everybody must answer truthfully except the murderer who may make up any story he likes. Naturally the dead body may not be interrogated!

Sardines

One player hides somewhere in the house or defined space, whilst the others count to forty. Then the hunt begins. The first person to find where the player is hiding has to squeeze in with her. The next one then squeezes in with them and so forth until everyone is packed into one place like sardines. The last person to find them becomes the next player to hide.

Consequences

This is a hilarious game for three or more players. Everyone is given a piece of paper and a pen and a basic plot line is decided and each step is written down. For example:

One *(type of day)* day
(A man's name) met *(a woman's name)*
With *(anything you like)*
At *(an event, place etc.)*

He said *(whatever he said)*
She said *(whatever she said)*
So they went *(a place, event, etc.)*
And *(something they did)*
And the consequence was *(whatever happened at the end)*

Each player writes down the man's name, folds the paper over so the next person can't see and passes it on to the person on his left. Then everyone writes a woman's name, folds it over and passes it to the person on the left etc. When everyone has finished, each person reads out their story.

This game can also be played with a poem. The first player writes three lines of a verse then folds the paper over so that the first two lines are hidden. She then passes it to the person on her left who writes another three lines, folding the paper over to hide all but the last line, and so on. The players can agree how many times the poem goes round or how many lines should be written and the last person reads the poem out to the others.

Pelmanism

Shuffle a pack of cards and lay out the whole pack face down. Each player in turn picks two cards and places them face upwards. If the two cards selected are two of a kind e.g. two Jacks or two tens, she removes them from the table and keeps them. She can then try again. If they are not two of a kind, the cards are replaced face down. Then the next player has her turn.

At first it is a game of chance but as the game progresses it becomes quite a feat of memory and the person at the end with the most cards wins.

Nicknames and Pseudonyms

(Answers on page 191)

You are really famous when the public knows you by a nick-name. Copy this list and hand a sheet to each player, or team of players, who must then fill in as many of the nickname owners as they can. It can be played against the clock or the players may be allowed to fill it in throughout the evening. This is a good game for dinner parties or quizzes as well. You could make up your own on a specific subject such as writers or pop stars.

	TEAM NAME	
1	The Young Pretender	
2	Coeur de Lion	
3	The Lady of the Lamp	
4	Bloody Mary	
5	The Virgin Queen	
6	The Old Lady of Threadneedle Street	
7	The Iron Chancellor	
8	The Iron Duke	
9	The Maid of Orleans	
10	The Welsh Wizard	
11	The Kingmaker	
12	Lewis Caroll	
13	The Waltz King	
14	The Gunners	
15	The City of the Seven Hills	
16	King Tut	
17	Satchmo	
18	The Boss	
19	The Big Apple	
20	The Confessor	
21	Scarface	
22	The Canaries	
23	The Unready	
24	Boz	
25	Acton Bell	
26	Isabel Mabarak Ripoll	

27	C S Lewis	
28	Currer Bell	
29	Stefani Joanna Angelina Germanotta	
30	Reginald Dwight	
31	George Orwell	
32	The Beast of Bolsover	
33	George Eliot	
34	Mark Twain	
35	Woody Allen	
36	Bono	
37	Elvis Costello	
38	Judy Garland	
39	Ben Kingsley	
40	Le Corbusier	
41	Meat Loaf	
42	Moby	
43	Mother Teresa	
44	Yves Saint-Laurent	
45	Ringo Starr	
46	Sid Vicious	
47	Fatboy Slim	
48	Oscar Wilde	
49	John Wayne	
50	The Iron Lady	

THINGS TO MAKE

Make a Tank that will Really Climb

This little tank can be made in a few moments.

The first thing you need is an empty wooden cotton reel and then you need to mark out teeth or cogs in the circular ends with a pencil and then cut them out with a sharp craft knife. Next, cut ½in/1.2cm off the bottom end of a candle, pull out the wick and make the hole slightly larger, making it perfectly round. Place the portion of the candle beside the reel and run a thin but strong elastic band through the centre of the two. Where the end of the loop projects through the reel, slip a matchstick and, where the end of the loop projects through the candle, slip a pencil about 3in/7.5cm.

Now hold the contrivance in one hand and with the other, twist the pencil round and round a number of times. This winds the elastic like a spring. When it is sufficiently wound, place the tank arrangement on the table and note its unusual movements. It will climb over such an obstacle as a small book with utmost ease.

Make Ginger Beer

Good ginger beer is a refreshing drink that you can make easily. Brewer's yeast can be bought at most health food shops and many supermarkets. This is how it's made:

Take one large lemon, peel it and cut the juicy parts into strips. Put this in a very large clean bowl or preserving pan and heap over it ¾lb/360g white granulated sugar, ½oz/15g of bruised ginger root and ¼oz/7g of cream of tartar.

Then pour about 6 pints of boiling water onto the ingredients and leave to cool. Then, when just warm, add a dessertspoonful of brewer's yeast. Leave it in a warm place for a day, then strain it through a muslin and pour into sterilized bottles. It is now ready for drinking but will last a long time if the bottles are clean and tightly stoppered.

Make a Pompom

Pompoms are great. You can use them to decorate a knitted beret or attach to slippers, or you can use them in numerous ways to make toys. You will need some thick card, a ten pence coin and some wool.

Cut two circles out of the card about 2½in/7cm in diameter. Draw a circle in the middle of each piece, using the ten pence coin as a template, then cut out the circles. Put the card rings together and start winding the wool round the outside and through the middle, round and round the rings until the centre is filled. It may help to use a blunt ended darning needle near the end.

Now cut the wool round the edges of the ring and pull the card rings slightly apart. Take a length of the same wool and wind it round the middle a few times, tying it off securely. Remove the card rings and fluff up your pompom. Trim off any uneven ends if you need to.

Now, let's take this a step further …

Make a Cotton Reel Caterpillar

Get a long piece of string, about 8 empty cotton reels, 2 small corks, paints and a paintbrush, some pipe cleaners cut in half, a darning needle and a pompom.

Paint the cotton reels and the corks whatever colour you want your caterpillar to be and leave them to dry.

Tie a knot in the end of the string and thread the other end through one of the corks, then through the cotton reels, and then through the middle of the pompom and finally through the second cork. Trim the string to the length you require.

Now take a pipe cleaner and wind the middle a couple of times round the string between the pompom and the first cotton reel to make legs. Then take another pipe cleaner and wind it round the string in between the first and second cotton reel and so on until you have lots of legs. You can trim them if you want them to be a little shorter.

And there you have your cotton reel caterpillar! You could try making other creatures with pompoms such as a spider with pipe cleaner legs or a mouse with felt ears and paws and a pipe cleaner for a tail.

Love's Farewell

Since there's no help, come let us kiss and part, –
Nay I have done, you get no more of me;
And I am glad, yea, glad with all my heart,
That thus so cleanly I myself can free;

Shake hands for ever, cancel all our vows,
And when we meet at any time again,
Be it not seen in either of our brows
That we one jot of former love retain.

Now at the last gasp of love's latest breath,
When, his pulse failing, passion speechless lies,
When faith is kneeling by his bed of death,
And innocence is closing up his eyes,

Now if thou would'st, when all have given him over,
From death to life thou might'st him yet recover!

Michael Drayton (1563–1631)

A Thunderstorm

The wind began to rock the grass
With threatening tunes and low, –
He flung a menace at the earth,
A menace at the sky.

The leaves unhooked themselves from trees
And started all abroad;
The dust did scoop itself like hands
And throw away the road.

The wagons quickened on the streets,
The thunder hurried slow;
The lightening showed a yellow beak,
And then a livid claw.

The birds put up the bars to nests,
The cattle fled to barns;
There came one drop of giant rain,
And then, as if the hands

That held the dams had parted hold,
The waters wrecked the sky,
But overlooked my father's house,
Just quartering a tree.

Emily Dickinson (1830–1886)

Cargoes

Quinquireme of Nineveh from distant Ophir
Rowing home to haven in sunny Palestine
With a cargo of ivory
And apes and peacocks.
Sandalwood, cedarwood, and sweet white wine.

Stately Spanish galleon coming from the isthmus,
Dipping through the Tropics by the palm-green shores,
With a cargo of diamonds,
Emeralds, amethysts,
Topazes, and cinnamon, and gold moidores.

Dirty British coaster with a salt-caked smoke stack
Butting through the Channel in the mad March days,
With a cargo of Tyne coal,
Road-rail, pig-lead,
Firewood, iron-ware, and cheap tin trays.

John Masefield (1878–1967)

Make a Viking Shield out of a Hub Cap

I noticed a few years ago how many hub caps from, presumably, bumped cars are left strewn about the roads, both in the town and the countryside and I was struck by how much they resembled Viking shields. I brought one home, washed it in hot soapy water and took off any obviously sharp bits. I found an old D-shaped drawer handle which I screwed on to the back and bingo! Ready for painting. Children can then spend a happy hour painting their shields and many happy hours fighting each other with a protective shield to reduce injuries.

What I actually did was to hold a party for Boy the Younger, where his friends were invited to come round dressed as Vikings. They spent an hour or so painting their shields, stopped for tea and games and then had free time to run around fighting each other. They had been instructed in advance to come tooled up! It was a huge success.

I find that acrylic paints work the best and are available in all good stationery and art supply shops. They cost about 99p a bottle but last for ages and can be used for all sorts of projects, including your own creative activities. Do wear an overall though, because although the paint washes off clothes if you get to it immediately, if it's left on, you've had it.

For the shield featured here, I did buy a pair of plastic handles for 99p from the DIY shop, but if you go to the tip or look around your neighbourhood for people with skips outside, you can usually find something suitable for nothing.

Any hub cap from a car will do but it must clean, dry and grease-free before you start

A simple drawer handle from the DIY shop or your own 'useful things drawer' will do the trick

Allow the first coat to dry thoroughly before applying further decoration

You may like to apply a coat of varnish when the design is completed

Just make two holes for the screws with a bradawl or drill and screw the handles on; it only takes 5 minutes.

Make Interesting Things with Matchboxes

Matchboxes make marvellous building materials and you can make almost anything out of them, from dolls house furniture to trucks, chopped off finger tricks to boxes for tiny things. Imagination is the main ingredient here.

You will generally need:

LOTS OF MATCHBOXES

SPLIT PINS

PAPER AND CARDBOARD

PAINTS – acrylics are best

PAINTBRUSH

SCISSORS

BRADAWL for making holes

GLUE

FELT, FABRIC SCRAPS, LACE AND WOOL Odds and ends that you think may be useful such as cotton reels, buttons etc.

Chest of Drawers

MATERIALS: 6 matchboxes, cardboard, paper, paints, split pins.

METHOD: Paste the boxes together, three high, two wide. Paste a piece of card on to the top of the chest, overlapping slightly. Paint the chest and the drawer fronts brown and leave to dry. Paint a thin gold line around the top of the chest and around each drawer. Make a hole in the middle of each drawer and push a split pin through, folding out the arms to make handles.

Matchbox chest of drawers – from *Practical Suggestions in Toymaking* (pre-war)

Bedstead

MATERIALS: 3 whole matchboxes and the cases of 2 others, paper, paint, bits of white fabric for sheets and pillows and other fabric or felt for a blanket. Needle and cotton. You may even want to knit a tiny blanket! Alternatively you could use a big box of Cook's Matches depending on how big you want it.

METHOD: Paste the 3 trays of boxes together and stick a strip of paper along them to make the mattress. Leave to dry. Make the head of the bedstead by pasting together two cases, and then pasting these at right angles, or on top of a third case. Next make the foot, by pasting one case at right angles to, and on top of, another case. Stick strips of paper or fabric round these pieces. The head and foot of the bed now have a little ledge on which to place the mattress. Paste this, hollow side

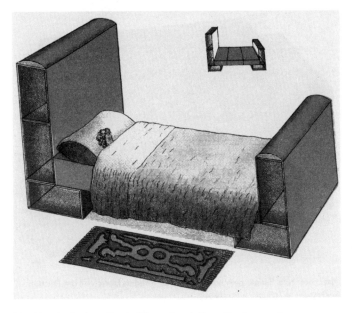

Matchbox bed – from *Practical Suggestions in Toymaking* (pre-war)

down onto the two ledges. Make tiny pillows stuffed with bits of felt or the fluff from the tumble dryer and sew them up. Cut pieces of white fabric for sheets and coloured fabric or a small piece of knitting for blankets.

A Comfy Sofa

MATERIALS: 8 whole matchboxes, some wooden beads for feet, felt for covering and cushions. A bit of lace for arm covers and antimacassars finished this off nicely.

METHOD: Glue 3 matchboxes together to form the seat, cover them in felt and leave to dry. Cover 2 single matchboxes in felt and leave to dry. Glue 2 matchboxes together lengthways, cover in felt and leave to dry. Meanwhile make some tiny cushions out of felt and cut out some scraps of lace to lay over

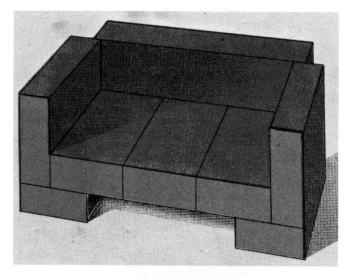

Matchbox sofa. Simple painted, but nicer covered in fabric – from *Practical Suggestions in Toymaking* (pre-war)

the arms and the back of the sofa. Now glue the single covered matchboxes at right angles to the seat to make arms. Then glue the long covered piece to the back to make the backrest. Hold them firmly and leave to dry. Glue or sew the lace to the sofa and arrange the little cushions.

A Tiny Train Set

MATERIALS: Lots of matchboxes, cardboard, buttons, split pins or pipe cleaners, spent matches, a little cotton wool.

METHOD: First make the locomotive. Glue two matchboxes together, glue in the trays, then paint or cover with coloured paper. Leave to dry. Now attach the tray of another matchbox to the back of the top boxes to make the cab. Glue a further box onto the back of this and put a cut away tray on top to make the tender. Paint it all to match or contrast with the front. Glue a tiny bobbin case or a small tube of card on to the

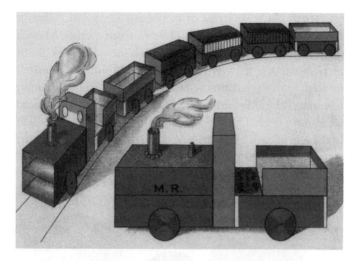

Matchbox train set. Well worth a bit of fiddly concentration – from *Practical Suggestions in Toymaking* (pre-war)

front to make the funnel and glue a little cotton wool to it to make steam. Attach buttons to the bottom for wheels and use matches to make the pistons. If you really want to be smart, mix some gravel, black paint and glue together and pour it into the tender to make the coal.

For the rest of the carriages use matchboxes to make trucks, passenger coaches and goods wagons, painting windows and doors as appropriate. Add matching buttons for the wheels. Link the coaches together with split pins or pipe cleaners.

TAKE IT FURTHER: Use further matchboxes to make a station platform and a bridge to go over the railway. Cardboard tunnels could be made and you could landscape the sides with green paint and little matchstick fences.

A Merry Go Round

MATERIALS: 2 empty cotton reels, the trays of 2 matchboxes, thick cardboard, a spent matchstick.

METHOD: Cut two strips of cardboard 8in x ⅜in/20cm x 1cm and glue them in the middle to form a cross. Make a small hole through the middle and push the matchstick about three quarters of the way through. Place the end of the match through one of the cotton reels and then glue the other cotton reel onto the cardboard cross making sure that the cardboard arms move freely. Cut the matchbox trays in half and glue half to the end of each of the arms. You can paint the arms and seats if you like to make them look jolly.

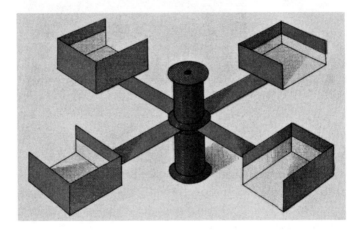

Matchbox merry go round – from *Practical Suggestions in Toymaking* (pre-war)

Make a Simple Jigsaw Puzzle

In an ideal world you could make this out of plywood and cut out the pieces with a fretsaw, but try this simpler method first and, when you are confident that you know the method, you can move on to making a large wooden puzzle first then graduating to smaller pieces. A homemade puzzle would make a lovely gift for a younger child or a relative with perhaps a photo of the family or their pet on it.

You will need:

An A4-sized piece of thick cardboard

An A4 picture – either a photograph, a photocopied picture or a page from a magazine

PVA glue

A pencil

A craft knife or very sharp scissors

METHOD: Cover the piece of cardboard with a thin, even layer of glue and attach the picture. Weigh the picture down with something heavy while it dries to keep it flat. When it is completely dry, turn it over and draw out your puzzle piece shapes with a pencil. Now cut out the shapes with a craft knife or scissors.

A Wooden Puzzle

If you then decide to progress to making a wooden puzzle, attach your picture with hot glue to make it really firm. Follow the instructions above but cut out the pieces very carefully with a fretsaw.

If you want to make it *really* hard, you can paste the same picture to both sides, but with one side at 180° or 90° rotation to the other. You will then either have to trace the puzzle piece shapes onto the picture or cut them out randomly as you go along.

Make Your Own Cards

Card making is a smashing way of being creative and giving something lovely and personal to people you like. Once again, we're back to our bag of scraps. If you are even remotely creative, you should always have a bag of scraps; coloured card, fabric, lace, bits of felt, ribbon, a folder or scrapbook in which to put cut-outs from magazines, newspapers and other cards. If you are given cards you particularly like for Christmas or your birthday, give them new life by cutting them out and making a collage card to give to someone else.

This jolly card was sent to me by my very creative friend Jenny Millard who handmakes cards for every occasion

Another thing you might want to consider is whether, if you're sticking lots of things on to make a 3D card, it will comply with the new post office width restrictions. I once received a beautiful handmade card from someone that was too thick for a 'letter' post and therefore had postage to pay. The postman took it away and I had to drive five miles to collect it and pay the difference. Rats!

If you have nice handwriting or can do calligraphy, that also makes a card look more special. You could use coloured inks, metallic or glitter pens. If you have rubbish handwriting you can buy stickers with nicely written greetings from craft and stationery shops.

You will need:
- Scissors/craft knife and/or small guillotine
- PVA glue which dries clear or a glue pen for ickle tiny things
- Paint brushes

METHOD: Start by deciding on the size of card – this might be determined by what size envelopes you have in stock. Look at the materials you have to hand and stare at them for some time, to see what comes in to your mind. Then think about whether the person is a more traditional type or a glittery and sparkly type, what is their sense of humour etc. Now get creative. Remember to leave each layer to dry thoroughly before adding the next and let the whole thing dry before posting.

Some Puzzles You Can Make

These puzzles and tricks can delight your friends at home or in the pub. Some of these puzzles can be done on paper; others are more robust if you attach them to plywood and can therefore be played again and again. The great thing about making diversions for yourself is that you have fun twice over – making the puzzle and then playing it!

Putting Down the Water Pipes

You will need:

A piece of plywood approximately 10 x 12in/
25 x 30cm, plus some offcuts
3 pieces of ribbon, wool or pipe cleaners in different
colours
Glue

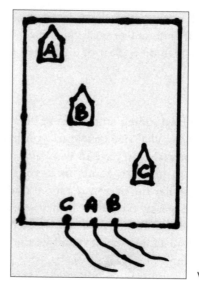

Water pipe puzzle

The drawing shows a plot of land on which stands three houses.
Each house needs a water supply and the water company has
informed the builder that the mains supply is located at C, A
and B as shown at the edge of the plot. Easy enough, you think,
but each house must be connected to its own supply (pipe A to
house A etc.) and none of the pipes must cross each other.

Make the puzzle out of the piece of thin plywood. Carve
the little houses out of the offcuts, and paint the whole thing
to look like houses on a plot of land. Place the houses and

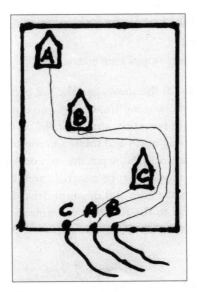

Water pipe puzzle solution

water mains as indicated on the drawing. Nail or glue pieces of ribbon or wool underneath the letters at the bottom. Leave to dry then torment your friends.

The Knife and Glasses Trick

You will need:

3 glass tumblers
3 dinner knives

Put the three glass tumblers on the table to form an equilateral triangle, slightly farther apart than the length of the knives. The trick is to arrange the three knives, the handle of each resting on the rim of the glasses and each supporting themselves in the centre.

SOLUTION: The end of the blade of each knife is placed so that it goes under the blade of one knife and over the blade of the other placed in the triangular pattern formed by the three knife blades.

189

The Coin and Drinking Straws Trick

You will need:

|| 5 drinking straws and a ten-pence piece

The trick is to lift the straws and the ten pence by holding only one end of one straw. 'Impossible!' you cry.

SOLUTION: Place two of the straws parallel on the table, about 3in apart, pointing north and south. On top of these lay two other straws diagonally. Now put the coin on top of the cross. The last straw should now be inserted carefully beneath the first straw, over the coin and down under the second straw which is parallel to the first. You can now carefully lift the whole lot off the table.

A Match Trick

You will need:

|| An empty matchbox, three unused matches, a lighter or more matches

Close the matchbox and stand it on its end. Insert a match, head up, into each side between the drawer and the case, about a quarter of the way in. Now put the third match horizontally between them so that it is wedged firmly, you may need to trim it slightly. Now ask your friends which of the two side matches will ignite first if you set fire to the match in the centre (lighting the middle). The trick is that either guess will be wrong as the centre match, when lighted, springs away as it burns leaving the side ones untouched.

Another Matchstick Puzzle

You will need:

|| 11 matchsticks

How can five more matches be added to six matches to make nine? I love this one.

Lay six matches vertically on the table, about two fingers width apart. Now add five matches to make nine.

Solution: Place the seventh match diagonally between the first two to form the letter 'N'. Place the eighth match diagonally between the fourth and fifth matches to form the second letter 'N'. Now use the last three to form an 'E' on the last match. This makes the word 'nine'. Cunning, huh?

ANSWERS TO NICKNAMES AND PSEUDONYMS

31	George Orwell	Eric Blair
32	The Beast of Bolsover	Dennis Skinner
33	George Elliot	Mary Anne Evans
34	Mark Twain	Samuel Langhorne Clemens
35	Woody Allen	Allan Stewart Konigsberg
36	Bono	Paul Hewson
37	Elvis Costello	Declan Patrick McManus
38	Judy Garland	Frances Ethel Gumm
39	Ben Kingsley	Krishna Banji
40	Le Corbusier	Charles Édouard Jeanneret
41	Meat Loaf	Marvin Lee Aday
42	Moby	Richard Hall
43	Mother Teresa	Agnes Gonxha Bojaxhiu
44	Yves Saint-Laurent	Henri Donat Mathieu
45	Ringo Starr	Richard Starkey
46	Sid Vicious	John Simon Ritchie
47	Fatboy Slim	Norman Cook
48	Oscar Wilde	Fingal O'Flahertie Wills
49	John Wayne	Marion Michael Morrison
50	The Iron Lady	Margaret Thatcher

	TEAM NAME	
1	The Young Pretender	Charles Edward Stuart
2	Coeur de Lion	King Richard I
3	The Lady of the Lamp	Florence Nightingale
4	Bloody Mary	Mary Tudor
5	The Virgin Queen	Queen Elizabeth I
6	The Old Lady of Threadneedle Street	The Bank of England
7	The Iron Chancellor	Bismark
8	The Iron Duke	The Duke of Wellington
9	The Maid of Orleans	Joan of Arc
10	The Welsh Wizard	David Lloyd-George
11	The Kingmaker	The Earl of Warwick
12	Lewis Caroll	Charles Dodgson
13	The Waltz King	Johann Strauss
14	The Gunners	Arsenal Football Club
15	The City of the Seven Hills	Rome
16	King Tut	Tutankhamen
17	Satchmo	Louis Armstrong
18	The Boss	Bruce Springsteen
19	The Big Apple	New York
20	The Confessor	King Edward I
21	Scarface	Al Capone
22	The Canaries	Norwich Football Club
23	The Unready	King Ethelred
24	Boz	Charles Dickens
25	Acton Bell	Anne Bronte
26	Isabel Mabarak Ripoll	Shakira
27	C S Lewis	Clive Hamilton
28	Currer Bell	Charlotte Bronte
29	Stefani Joanna Angelina Germanotta	Lady Gaga
30	Reginald Dwight	Elton John

FELINE KILLING MACHINES AND HOW I LEARNED TO LOVE ONE

Some years ago, a thin, manky little coal black cat appeared in our hallway. She wandered in, looked around the house, miaowing piteously all the while and finally climbed onto my shoulders and drooled gently down my neck.

I am obliged to point out that this is not good for several reasons. Firstly, I am asthmatic. Secondly, I am allergic to cats. Thirdly, the merest puncture from a cat's claw has me up in red wheals that itch like billy-oh for a minimum of two hours. Lastly, but not leastly, I don't like cats. I am a renowned cat-hater of this parish. I am a dog person who likes all dogs indiscriminately and harbours lurking misgivings about my friends and family who keep cats for pleasure.

She was, however, clearly half starved so I gave her some scraps and a little warm milk which she devoured in seconds. She then curled up on the sofa and went to sleep. The next morning she woke up, had more scraps and crapped in Boy the Younger's bedroom. 'Please let us keep her, please, please,' wailed the boys. 'No,' I said firmly, 'Her owners are probably missing her dreadfully, we are about to move house, she is clearly not house trained and I don't like cats.' This was not deemed to be a reasonable excuse.

I gave her every opportunity to leave, I left doors open and stared at her in a nasty way. I did all the things one is supposed to do: I asked all the neighbours, I put up some posters and I took her to the vet to see if she had been chipped. She hadn't and the vet said that she was little more than a kitten, generally healthy and that it was very common for country cats to snuggle down in the back of horse boxes then wake up 50 miles from home, lost and lonely. 'Lost. And Lonely,' crooned the vet with glittering eyes. Oh crap.

How prescient. Over the next week, she relentlessly crapped in every corner of the bedroom and began weeing on the beds for good measure. Still, at least I discovered where the launderette was in Market Harborough and the quilts probably needed freshening up anyway. I had earmarked the £25 I eventually spent there for other fripperies like food, but cat wee smells like nothing else on earth and it was marginally cheaper than buying new duvets. All the while I was trying to pack up the extensive contents of my house, ready to move. Every time I bent down, she would leap at me and sit on my neck while I tried to work, using needle-like claws as crampons on the Helvellyn of my back, my contorted shoulders providing her very own Striding Edge upon which to torment me.

We moved on 1 April. How apt. Realising that she was clearly not litter trained, I bought a litter tray which is the most revolting object in existence. One day, remind me to fill you in on the comparative merits of cat litter brands – I know them all. I made absolutely no attempt to keep Smog (oh – didn't I mention that we'd named her?) but she resolutely refused to leave and to add insult to injury, she was getting rather fat. I'd never owned a cat so the natural assumption was that I was overfeeding her and Smog was put on a diet.

The attacks started almost immediately and a few days later, as I was conversing pleasantly with my new neighbour, she said cheerfully 'I see your cat's in the family way!' 'What?!' I spluttered through a mouthful of truly horrid expletives. Surely I must have noticed? Fat tummy, nipples, huge appetite, sleeping more, reluctance to go out etc. No. I had not noticed. I have never had a cat. I do not like cats, particularly teenage, runaway, ASBO, pregnant cats. Her food was reinstated and a moral lecture was administered, with the threat of the Magdalene Laundries left hanging in the air.

The 26 of April was a Sunday. For the Wartime Housewife, this means as long a sleep as the boys will allow, followed by coffee in bed whilst listening to *The Archers*. Smog waddled into the room and sat on my shoulder. She isn't normally allowed in the bedrooms (not with her record) but I was feeling magnanimous and mellow, so tolerated her warm little body against my ear.

I don't know what made me look, but suddenly I turned my head and there was a tiny, soggy, black and white 'thing' the size of a hamster, lying on my pillow. An ejector seat mysteriously appeared in my bed and I ran round the house calling for hot water, soap and towels, but by the time the towels appeared, she had already popped out another one. Another trip to the launderette loomed large.

Over the next two hours, Smog silently presented us with five black and white kittens. I have never seen an animal give birth and, other than the immediate eating of the placental sacks, I was rather envious of the ease and naturalness with which it all occurred. The news spread like wildfire and I had a constant stream of local children filing through my bedroom, examining the kittens while I sat slightly awkwardly in my pyjamas like some historical duchess granting audience in my chamber.

Smog was an excellent mother. She and the kittens had a house made out of a cardboard box with a blanket in it and all was well. Until their eyes opened and they started to move. It became a full time job just trying to keep them all in the house as doors were constantly left open and they wandered out into the lane where they were abducted by the hoards of children surrounding the house at all hours. She trained them to use the litter tray but it was always full and stinking and horrible. I loathed them, and at the first opportunity, an advert was drafted, to at least recoup the vast amount of money spent on food, litter and cleaning materials, to say nothing of the increase in the consumption of London Gin.

To cut a long story short, all five kittens were eventually sold. A friend, with more courage than wisdom suggested that Smog had given me the 'gift of kittens' as a thank you for taking her in. As soon as they were gone, she settled down, stopped needing the litter tray and became her old cuddly self. She grew significantly over the next few months, her coat thick and gleaming, her habits fastidious. And she got spayed, thanks to the Cats Protection League.

But then she turned into a killing machine. I kicked her outside in the morning and brought her in at night (as naturalists implore us to do) but every afternoon, I found at least two mice outside the dining room window, she frequently took-out wood pigeons and had been witnessed murdering large rabbits in the meadow. If only she'd take the trouble to learn to skin them, I thought, it would be a culinary partnership made in heaven and I would have loved her even more. She went missing for three days one month (on a serial killing rampage, no doubt) and I was nearly sick with anxiety.

Now, as I write, she is draped across my shoulders, purring loudly into my ear and gently clawing my back. Strangely, I don't seem to be as allergic any more.

6

GARDENING

To start you off, here is a brief glossary of gardening terms:

ANNUALS – These are plants which live for one season only and have to be planted every year. Obviously you can save the seed to grow on next year

BIENNIALS – These plants only last two years, meaning that you sow them one year and they flower the next. Again, save the seeds

PERENNIALS – These plants die down at the end of their season each year but always come up again the following spring

DECIDUOUS – These are trees and bushes which shed all their leaves in the autumn

EVERGREEN – These trees and bushes keep their leaves all through the winter

HALF HARDY – This means plants that should be kept protected from cold and frost

HARDY – These plants should withstand most British winters as long as the weather isn't extreme

HERBACEOUS – These plants are perennial but die down to the root each year

SHRUBS – These are larger bushy plants which are perennial

GENERAL TIPS

- Do everything you can to improve the vitality and structure of your **soil**.
- **Keep records** of what you do, whether it's a complicated rotation scheme or your hanging baskets. Include photographs. This is how you learn and improve.
- Before doing muddy gardening, scrape your fingernails across a bar of soap. When you come to **wash your hands**, the dirt will wash away without staining.
- When you **buy bulbs**, make sure that they are cultivated and not gathered from the wild.
- Don't overstretch yourself. Think about your other commitments and plan your gardening accordingly. If you have too much to do, gardening will become **outdoor housework** instead of a pleasure.

Weeding women, *Housewife Magazine*

- Don't be hidebound by experts. **Experiment** and see what works; if you like it, try it.
- Tights or stockings can make gentle but strong **plant ties** as they are firm but stretch to accommodate growth.
- **Mothballs** hung in peach trees will prevent leaf curl and are a cheaper alternative to Bordeaux mixture.
- Always give new plants a good drink before planting – when you move house the first thing you want is a cup of tea. Plants are the same.
- Cut the feet off **old wellies** to make arm guards for when you're pruning roses or pyrocantha.
- Learn the benefits of **companion planting** to save on pesticides and weedkillers.
- Think about **planting a hedge** rather than a fence as this will provide extra habitats for wildlife. If you must have a fence, leave small gaps for hedgehogs and toads to creep through.
- Work with **nature**, not against it.
- Only plant a **walnut tree** if you have a really big garden. They are very beautiful but are bad news for neighbouring plants as the walnut contains a chemical which can have a toxic effect on other plants if it enters the soil.
- Retrieve windows from builders' skips and use them to make **cold frames**.
- Lily of the Valley enjoys being fed with water that has been mixed with a couple of tablespoons of **soot**. Leeks will grow stronger if you add two or three handfuls of soot to the soil when you plant them.
- **Old net curtains** make excellent protective nets for soft fruit and protect espaliered plants from frost.
- If you are planting for the new season or moving your garden around, try to have an area with a bit of hedge where **insects and small animals** can shelter. Also reserve a small area which can go a bit wild, including some logs to encourage beetles and suchlike.

- Choose plants that will actively **encourage wildlife** to keep your garden in natural balance.
- Put broken crocks in the bottom of plant pots to increase **drainage**.
- Line pottery pots with bubble wrap before filling up with soil. This helps to prevent **pots cracking** in cold weather.
- Don't throw away old feather filled pillows. Soak the feathers in a bucket of water and then dig them into your soil over the winter at a rate of about 6oz/180g to the square m/yd to provide **slow-release nitrogen**.
- Scatter **broken eggshells** round the base of plants; not only will it deter slugs but they enhance the colour of roses.
- **Banana skins** planted under rose bushes will ensure a fabulous display of flowers.
- If your grass is desperate for a good mowing but is very wet, walk up and down the lawn with a rake and bash the grass with it. This knocks all the **water off the grass** onto the soil and allows you to mow with ease.

CLOCHES

A cloche was originally a glass bell jar, although they can be made from almost anything. They are used to protect growing plants from wind, rain and frost and to make the most of the sun's rays and retain some of its heat. They are effectively a miniature greenhouse. A poly-tunnel is just a great big cloche. In colder areas of the country, the growing season can be extended by the use of cloches and means that one can sow earlier as well.

They also help to protect against pests and diseases, particularly in hot dry periods.

It is important that they should have ventilation. For small plants a cut off pop bottle can be used and you can adjust the ventilation by unscrewing the cap. For larger cloches you need to have removable panes.

'How to Dig'. Booklet issued by The Ministry of Agriculture as part of a series encouraging home food production

DIG FOR VICTORY LEAFLET
NUMBER 20   (NEW SERIES)
ISSUED BY THE MINISTRY OF AGRICULTURE

CONTAINER GARDENING

I was recently waxing lyrical to my friends about the ease and virtue of growing vegetables in pots. I love home grown vegetables but sometimes there are simply not enough hours in the day to be digging and composting, improving the soil followed by yet more digging and raking. Sometimes there is more to life than a fine tilth.

The easy and effective solution to this is to grow vegetables in pots. One can grow practically anything in a pot and the great benefit of this type of gardening is that each pot can contain a completely different soil type to get the best out of your veg.

Carrots like poor, sandy soil, so a big pot of earth mixed with sharp sand will produce a fine crop.

Cauliflowers like rich, firm, deep soil whilst onions and garlic will grow in practically anything as long as the soil is well-drained.

A dustbin full of soil can produce half a dozen corn on the cobs.

Beans and peas (legumes) prefer a rich, light, slightly limey soil and don't like the cold.

Even better, crop rotation is easy, as all you have to do is change pots. I always keep a notebook in which I write details of what I've planted in each pot and this allows for a bit of experimentation. It is important not to grow the same plants in the same soil as the soil will become depleted and prone to disease.

Also, always remember to wash pots out before re-use to avoid spreading disease.

There is also much scope for companion planting as you don't have to use up valuable veg growing space with flowers.

- Simply pop a pot of marigolds next to your carrots to repel aphids and carrot root fly – onions also repel carrot fly
- Oregano fends off cabbage white butterflies
- Sage is a deterrent against flea beetles, slugs and cabbage moth
- Give it a go and pop in a few onion sets and spuds and see how you get on. Seed packets and small plants (sets) nearly always have clear instructions on how close plants should be and it may be that you just plant one cabbage to a pot, or a couple of seed potatoes.

But vegetables aside, container planting is simple and effective. My front garden is just a path and a bit of gravel really and yet I have made a display of flowers planted in all sorts of containers including stone jars, an old watering can, stacked defunct hanging baskets and an awful lot of boots and shoes.

Old boots make fabulous pots because they're porous and the leather has useful nutrients. I have a run of shoes full of alpines, which are quite happy in shallower soil but also make a rather nice and somewhat literal stepping stone effect across the gravel.

However you choose to garden, use your imagination and don't be constrained by what is conventional or recommended. Have fun.

GARDEN PONDS

A garden pond is a great way of attracting wildlife to your garden including dragonflies, frogs, toads and hedgehogs. It doesn't have to be of epic proportions, the location is the most important thing to consider. However, a larger pond is easier to keep clean. It should be in a quiet part of the garden, free from the shadows of tall trees or fences – the roots of trees can disrupt the liner apart from anything else.

The pond should have a minimum depth of 18in/45cm and ideally have a deep end of about 30in/80cm so that creatures can hibernate away from the frost. A pond lined with plastic sheeting is the easiest and cheapest method of proceeding. Fibreglass liners are useful but are too shallow for fish.

When you have dug your pond, allow a couple of weeks for the liner to settle in before starting the planting.

Planting

For the deep end you should have lilies, floating plants and oxygenating plants. For the shallow end and marginal zone there are many plants that are happy in very shallow water indeed. Arrowheads, irises, water forget-me-nots and marsh marigolds are all ideal.

Allow one oxygenating plant for every square m/yd of pond surface.

Water lilies will need to be lifted and divided every three years or they will take over.

If you want to introduce frogs and toads into your garden get in touch with your local wildlife trust who will advise you where to get spawn. Do not add spawn to a pond with fish as the fish will, will malice aforethought, just eat them all.

HANGING BASKETS

- Old jumpers make good and colourful liners for hanging baskets
- Old carpet offcuts also make good liners
- Old sponges and rags can be placed in hanging baskets to hold water
- You can line a hanging basket with used tea bags which not only hold water but help to fertilise as well

THE JOY OF CHICKENS

Chickens are a complete pleasure to have in the garden and even a small garden can support a couple of birds. They look lovely, they sound nice and comforting, and they lay eggs. They are easy to keep and you can feed them all sorts of scraps.

Do check with your neighbours that they are happy for you to keep chickens, particularly if you fancy a cockerel as they can be noisy critters and a pain in the neck. Also, if you rent your house, check with your landlord that you are allowed to keep them as some tenancies prohibit the keeping of livestock.

There is a huge choice of breeds to choose from and you will need to get some advice as to whether a specific breed is what you need or whether you want to rescue some former intensively reared hens that will still lay and will love you forever.

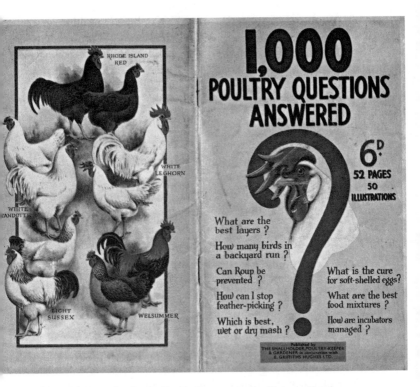

Useful booklet by *The Smallholder, Gardener and Poultry- Keeper*; undated

Chickens don't need a huge amount of space but they will turn whatever patch you give them into mud, so if you keep them in a run, you will need to move it frequently to allow the grass to recover and to avoid the build up of parasites.

The hen house can be a simple affair as chickens only want two things; somewhere to roost at night and somewhere to lay her eggs. You need to be able to access the eggs from outside and to be able to clean the inside of the hen house periodically.

Chicken feed has to be stored where vermin can't get at it. They will need a regular supply of layers' pellets or meal if you want them to lay eggs daily. Grain should only be given in the afternoon and no more than 1oz/30g per bird. I would suggest feeding them in the morning so that rats are not attracted to the coop during the night.

Step-on feeders or hanging feeders are a good idea as the hens can feed at will, the pellets are kept dry and help to prevent our long tailed friends from getting their noses in the trough.

Chickens are woodland creatures by nature and they love to climb up things, roost up high to get away from predators and to scratch around in grass and scrub for food.

You don't need a cockerel if you don't want chicks. This may seem obvious but there are pros and cons to cockerels. They are good at keeping a harem of hens in order and protecting them from harm. Sometimes you are considered the predator, so they may go for you and they can be quite fierce.

If you do have chicks, remove the male birds as soon as you can or the cockerels will fight for supremacy and it isn't pretty. Ideally, eat the surplus male birds.

Chickens don't need a lot of medical treatment, but they will need to be wormed, de-loused and be given preventative treatment for red spider mite and scaly legs/feet. There are lots of products on the market that do this job easily without you needing to visit the vet.

MULCHING, COMPOSTING AND MANURING

- Strips of carpet also make an excellent mulch to rid a strip of ground of weeds. Old lino or vinyl flooring are equally good.
- Grow bags can be used again in several ways. They can be used to store root vegetables over winter. They can be put into a corner of the garden and sown with flower seeds for cutting and drying. You can also use the compost for spring flowering bulbs and for mulching around new shrubs.

▼

- Encourage the male members of your family to wee on the compost heap. This acts as an activator and gives them a good excuse for peeing outdoors which they seem to want to do anyway.
- Thick grass cuttings round the bottom of raspberry canes bring them on a treat.
- Make manure go further by mixing it with grass cuttings or straw. The litter from rabbits, guinea pigs or chickens is ideal.
- Manure should be kept dry and turned regularly to prevent it heating up too much. Cover with plastic sheeting, lino or a sheet of corrugated iron to stop the rain washing away valuable nutrients.
- Old dustbins make ideal compost bins. Turn them upside down and remove the bottom. The lid can then be used to cover it and the compost removed by just tipping the bin up.
- Bury old leather boots underneath peach trees, close to the roots to encourage good growth.
- Chicken poo increases the size of your plums.
- Newspaper laid between rows of plants and then covered with straw will provide excellent weed control.
- A flame gun is a great way of controlling weeds without chemicals, especially on patios.
- Beans need very nutritious soil. Ask your hairdresser to keep all the hair sweepings at the end of the day and line your prepared trenches with it before sowing.

Leaflet 26 issued by the Ministry of Agriculture: 'How to use Cloches'

NETTLES

Nettles are your friends. Always leave a patch of ground on which to grow them. Not only are they a nutritious vegetable, but you can use them in the following ways:

- Plunge the tough stalks into boiling water to get rid of the sting and soften them, then use them as natural ties for plants.
- Keep your patch well away from your veggies and they should attract butterflies and caterpillars as a decoy.
- Nettles are a folk remedy for arthritis: pick a large fresh bunch and whip it against the affected joints. This stimulates the adrenal glands and reduces the swelling.
- Boil half a carrier bag of nettles in four pints of water and then leave to infuse for at least three days. Strain off the liquid and spray as an insecticide. I believe this also deters moles but I wouldn't swear to it.

PEST CONTROL

- To catch snails before they eat your stuff, put some bran on the ground then cover it with cabbage leaves. The snails will creep under the leaves where you can catch them and release them into someone else's garden or the local snail sanctuary (or stomp on them – whatever). Alternatively, put your snails in a tank of sweet salad leaves for a week to cleanse their little systems, then eat them. No, really.
- Try to encourage hedgehogs into your garden as they thrive on slugs, wireworms, cutworms and grubs. Don't be too tidy. Leave wild areas and maybe a small pile of logs or brushwood and dry leaves. This will also attract interesting beetles and other wildlife. If you build fences or walls, leave small holes in overgrown corners for hedgehogs to get in and out. If hedgehogs start visiting, a tiny bit of meaty cat food or muesli mixed with water in a dish will encourage them, and water will be welcome in hot weather. Hedgehogs don't care what their food tastes like but, believe it or not, you can buy

cans of hedgehog food called 'Spike's Dinner', but research into that is down to you. Do not, however, give them bread and milk – it's very bad for them.

- Spread soot from your fire around plants to deter slugs.
- Attract predators. For example, marigolds planted between rows of brassicas attract hoverflies and parasitic wasps, which eat mealy aphids and young cabbage white caterpillars.
- Deter cats by sprinkling lemongrass or eucalyptus essential oil onto tea bags and leave them round your flower beds.
- Garlic cloves placed in rose bushes will help to keep them aphid free.
- Moisten seedlings with a little paraffin before planting to deter mice and birds.
- Spray aphids with washing up water or soapy water.
- Put a mixture of sour milk and lemon juice into the middle of your growing cabbages weekly to discourage caterpillars.
- Grow marigolds next to your carrots to repel aphids and carrot root fly – onions also repel carrot fly.
- Sawdust soaked in paraffin and laid in trails will also prevent carrot fly.
- Push the seedlings of brassicas through a square of tarred roofing felt when planting in the ground to deter cabbage root fly.

'How to Sow Seeds'. Booklet issued by The Ministry of Agriculture as part of a series encouraging home food production

- Lavender bags hung among your plants will help deter moths in the garden as well as in your wardrobe.
- Oregano fends off cabbage white butterflies.
- Sage is a deterrent against flea beetles, slugs and cabbage moth.
- Mix baking yeast and sugar and place it on bits of bark around plants or trees that need to be protected from ants.
- Ants also hate chalk and cayenne pepper.
- Boil a pan of green potatoes, strain off the liquid and use as an all purpose repellent and insecticide.
- ... and a shotgun soon sorts out the squirrels. I jest of course – a catapult is far less ostentatious.

SAVING WATER

- Save water at every possible opportunity – don't stop at having a water butt; grey water can be used all over the place.
- Use water from hot water bottles and kettles to water indoor plants or hanging baskets.
- Washing up water can be poured onto patios to help control weeds.
- Cooking water from vegetables or fish can be used to water plants and add extra nutrients.
- Use the water from your fish tank to water plants, inside and out.
- Use a spray gun rather than a watering can to water seedlings as it uses less water and is less likely to crush the shoots.

SEEDS AND SOWING

- After sowing seeds, put a stick into the ground at the end of the row then place the seed packet or a label into a jam jar and put it upside down onto the stick.
- Sow the seeds of thirsty plants into trenches lined with newspaper.

- Individual seeds can be planted in tea bags and kept moist. When they sprout they can be transferred directly into the soil without upsetting the roots.
- Seedlings can be protected from pests with plastic bottles, using the end with the cap on so you can allow air in.
- Always store seeds in paper bags, in a dry temperate place, away from vermin.
- If you want to grow seeds on on a windowsill but don't want the seedlings to become leggy in the sun, make a light focus box out of cardboard that is taller at the back, tapering to a low front. Line the back and sides with tin foil. The reflected light will help the seedlings grow strong without leaning towards the window.
- Plastic milk cartons, cut in half, make very effective cloches for young plants. You can adjust air flow through the lid.
- Always sow seeds at the time of the waxing moon. This aligns the sowing with the rhythmic powers exerted by the moon. Surprisingly, this isn't bollocks and if you grow a lot of vegetables it's worth investing in a moon planting guide.
- Moisten seedlings with a little paraffin before planting to deter mice and birds.
- If you're not sure when to risk planting your seeds outside, test the temperature of the soil with your elbow; if it feels pleasant, it's warm enough to sow.
- Mix small seeds with flour and water paste or wallpaper paste and sew them using an icing bag. This will ensure even, straight sowing.
- If you are sowing peas, beans or larger seed and you're not sure whether it's past its best, pour a handful into a bowl of water and shake it up a bit. The good seeds will sink and the less good will float on the top.
- A rather lovely way of growing beans is to train them up against sunflowers. Plant your sunflowers as early as possible to allow good growth. When they are about two feet high, sow three bean plants at the foot of each sunflower.
- Improve seed potatoes by removing all but the two strongest sprouts. These should ideally be under 2in long.
- Many bedding plants will self-seed if you let them. Instead of dead heading all the plants, let some of them go to seed. Then in the autumn shake the seeded plants into your flower beds. These can then be potted up and taken indoors for the winter. They can then be replanted in the spring.

STORING SURPLUS CROPS

With the best will in the world you can't eat everything as it matures in the garden. Some of it will need to be stored. Freezers are the great friend of the modern gardener and many fruits and vegetables can be successfully frozen for long-term storage.

However, most winter vegetables can be stored without freezing. Carrots, apples, potatoes, pears, onions, parsnips, swedes all store very well over winter. It is important to make sure that stored produce is not damaged or it will rot and spoil the other things.

- Carrots and parsnips can be left in the ground, but it is prudent to cover them with straw to keep the hardest frosts at bay.
- Potatoes store best in hessian or thick paper sacks. Make sure that they are not damaged. Keep them in the dark and in a frost-free place – cover them with old blankets if necessary. If any start to sprout, remove enough to use for your seed crop the following year.
- Onions should be hung up in strings or plaits in a cool damp place. Garlic should be stored in strings and put in a warm place such as near the boiler.
- Root crops should not be washed before storage. Allow them to dry off after you've lifted them and trim off any leaves just above the neck. Carrots, swedes and parsnips should be stored in sand or the used soil from growbags. They should be layered in deep wooden boxes with the larger ones at the bottom and stored in a cool place.
- Peas and beans are well suited to freezing although runner beans fare best when salted and kept in a large crock.
- Apples should be wrapped in oiled paper wraps (butter papers are good for this) and placed in wooden storage trays in a dark, airy, humid place. Apples actually freeze quite nicely but they must be peeled, cored, sliced and blanched before you do it.

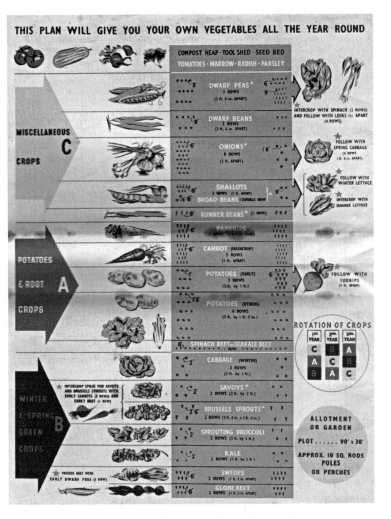

Dig for Victory growing plan, Leaflet I issued by the Ministry of Agriculture

- Pears are best stored unwrapped but must be placed so that they are not touching each other. They will not keep as long as apples and bottling may be a better option.
- Soft fruit and berries do not keep well and you are better off freezing them or making jam or compotes.
- Plums, cherries and peaches are likewise better bottled and stored.

TABLE OF PLANTING AND PERIOD OF USE

WINTER AND EARLY SPRING SUPPLIES PRINTED IN GREEN

CROP	TIME OF SOWING	DISTANCE APART		PERIOD OF USE
		Rows	Plants	
BEANS (Broad)	Feb.-March	1 double row	6 in. by 9 in.	July
BEANS (Dwarf)	Late April-Early May	2½ ft.	9 in.	July-Aug.
BEANS (Dry Haricot) ..	Late April-Early May	2½ ft.	9 in.	Winter
BEANS (Runner)	Mid-May		9 in.	July-Oct.
BEET	(1) April (2) June	15 in.	6 in. (thin)	July-April
BROCCOLI (Sprouting) ..	Mid-May Plant Mid-July	2 ft.	2 ft.	Feb.-May
BRUSSELS SPROUTS ..	March Plant May-June	2½ ft.	2½ ft.	Nov.-Mar.
CABBAGE (Spring) ..	July-August Plant Sept.-Early Oct.	1½ ft.	1½ ft.	April-Jan.
CABBAGE (Winter) ..	Mid.-May Plant Mid.-July	2 ft.	2 ft.	
CABBAGE (Cold Districts)	April	1½ ft.	1½ ft.	Autumn
CARROTS (Early) ..	April	1 ft.	6 in. (thin)	June-Sept.
CARROTS (Maincrop) ..	June-Early July	1 ft.	6 in. (thin)	Oct.-May
KALE	May Plant Mid.-July	2 ft.	2 ft.	Jan.-April
LEEKS	March Plant July	1 ft.	6 in. 9 in.	Mar.-May
LETTUCE (Summer) ..	March and every 14 days	Between other crops	9 in.	May-Oct.
LETTUCE (Winter Hardy)	Sept.	1 ft.	9 in.	Spring
MARROW	May		3-4 ft.	July-Feb.
ONIONS	Mid.-Feb.	1 ft.	6 in. (thin)	July-June
PARSNIPS	Mid.-Feb.-Mid.-March	15 in.	6 in. (thin)	Nov.-Mar.
PEAS (Early) .. PEAS (Others) ..	March and April	2½ ft.	3 in.	June-July
POTATOES (Early) ..	March	2 ft.	1 ft.	July-Aug.
POTATOES (Others) ..	April	2 ft.	1 ft. 3 in.	Sept.-Mar.
RADISHES..	March onwards	1 ft.		May-June
SAVOY	Late May Plant July-Aug.	2 ft.	2 ft.	Jan.-Mar.
SHALLOTS	February	1 ft.	6 in.	Jan.-Dec.
SPINACH (Summer) ..	Mid.-April	1 ft.	6 in. (thin)	Summer
SPINACH (Winter) ..	Sept.	1 ft.	6 in. (thin)	Spring
SPINACH BEET .. or SEAKALE BEET ..	April	8 in.	8 in. (groups)	July-Oct. and Jan.-June
SWEDES	End June	15 in.	6 in. (thin)	Dec.-Mar.
TOMATOES	Plant end May		15 in.	Aug.-Oct.
TURNIP (Roots) ..	July	1 ft.	6 in. (thin)	Oct.-Mar.
TURNIP (Tops) ..	End August	1 ft.	Sow thinly	April

Printed for H.M. Stationery Office by T. G. Porter (Printers) Ltd., Leeds. 51-1782.

Dig for Victory planting guide, Leaflet I issued by the Ministry of Agriculture

WINDOW BOX AND ROOF GARDENING

People with no garden can still grow food and flowers. Many apartment blocks have flat roofs which are perfect for container gardening but if you have no roof, there are still window boxes.

Crops that can be easily grown on roofs include tomatoes, lettuce, beans, radishes, cucumbers, pumpkins, squash, gherkins, marrows, cabbage, onions, carrots, beetroot, garlic and useful kitchen herbs such as mint, parsley, thyme and sage as well as strawberries, raspberries and many varieties of patio fruit trees. Sweetcorn can be grown very successfully in dustbins.

Crops suitable for window boxes are more limited but lettuce, radishes, tomatoes, dwarf beans and strawberries can all be grown successfully.

Save space by choosing varieties of a medium habit of growth, which, whilst taking up less room often crop just as well as the more robust kinds.

Roof gardens and window boxes are often higher than ground level and therefore more exposed and colder, so the aspect is very important. There must be protection from north and east winds and preferably face south or west to afford the maximum amount of sunlight. But as long as you provide some draught exclusion and perhaps a cloche or two, it is still possible to grow good things.

How to begin – Soil must be held compactly in strong containers. It must be rich and appropriate to the crop. You will need to water far more often, taking care not to over-water and the plants will need safe and adequate drainage.

Care of plants – Strong supports will be needed for tomatoes or beans and plants must be fastened firmly to those supports. Remember to leave plenty of room for growth and have spare pots ready for when you thin out seedlings. Make sure you eat vegetables as they come to maturity in order to make room for the crops that follow on.

7

HEALTH AND BEAUTY

Health and beauty are inextricably linked, but we don't have to spend out fortunes on personal trainers and fashionable cosmetics to achieve both things. Healthy food, plenty of sleep and exercise will do as much to make you gorgeous as all the potions on the shelves.

I'm not going to bang on about the things you must eat and the minimum number of miles you must jog each day to keep fit because you know all that stuff; either you do it already and feel understandably smug or you feel you don't have the time or the energy and feel guilty.

I seem to remember a naval manual for dealing with a shipwreck which read, 'No 1: Do not get yourself into this situation,' (or somesuch teeth-gnashingly self-righteous statement). Of course we should all look after ourselves because we are very important, both to ourselves and to those who rely on us. We should go to bed early, always have breakfast, drink lots of water, not drink too much alcohol, watch our fat and carbohydrate, take regular exercise and not get cross.

But no matter how hard we try, life has a nasty habit of sticking its grubby fingers up in a most un-gentlemanly way and we fall by the wayside. Coupled with that, what

would life be without wine, chocolate, Badger Beers, late nights, the odd scrap and the occasional Marlboro red?

So here are some easy home remedies, simple exercises and beauty tips.

STIES

Just for interest, the official name for a sty is 'hordeolum', which sounds suspiciously like a bedding plant to me ...

What you need:
- 1 medium sized bowl
- 2 drops lavender essential oil
- 2 drops chamomile essential oil
- 1 clean flannel

Method:

Wash your hands very thoroughly.

Pour some boiling water into the bowl and leave it until it is hot enough to put your hands in.

Put in 2 drops of lavender and 2 drops of chamomile essential oil and stir well.

Put the flannel into the water in readiness.

If possible, find the eyelash sticking out of the pustule and try to pull it out.

If you can't do this, pull your eyelid out with one hand and apply pressure to the pustule with the other. The pus should come out quite easily.

Even if it doesn't, wring out the flannel and immediately apply it to your *closed* eye.

When the flannel has cooled, put it back in the hot water, wring it out and apply again.

Keep doing this until the water has cooled. Put it in the fridge.

When the water is cold, wring out the flannel and apply it to your *closed* eye.

Do this for about 10 minutes, then put the bowl back in the fridge.

After an hour, do it again.

Keep repeating this process until you go to bed. *Early*.

GARGLE FOR A SORE THROAT

What you need:
- 1 small bottle or jam jar – very clean
- 3 tablespoons cider vinegar
- 1 tablespoon honey
- 3 drops ginger essential oil
- 5 drops lemon essential oil
- 2 drops thyme essential oil

Method:

Blend well and mix 1 tablespoonful of the mixture into a tumbler of warm water and gargle energetically. *Do not swallow.* Put the remaining mixture into the jam jar and seal tightly. Repeat ever two hours.

MOUTHWASH FOR HEALTHY GUMS

What you need:
- Tincture of myrrh – available from chemists
- Peppermint essential oil

Method:

Put one drop of each into a small glass of warm water and rinse out your mouth. *Do not swallow.*

Use daily.

INDIGESTION, ACID REFLUX, BLOATING, WIND

Get a large handful of fresh mint leaves or a flat tablespoon of dried mint and put into a jug or teapot.

Pour over about ¾ pint of boiling water.

Leave to infuse for about 10 minutes.

Strain and sip gently and slowly until it is all gone.

Repeat when necessary.

You can also use peppermint essential oil if you have it. Two drops to 1 pint of very hot water, stir well and pour out the required amount into a glass. Sip gently until completely gone.

PERFECT FOOD FOR UPSET TUMS

If you have had a nasty stomach upset and are at the point where you need something to eat but can't think of a single thing you want, eat this:

¼ pint of natural live (probiotic) yoghurt
1 big tablespoon pure honey
½ ripe banana – sliced

The yoghurt helps to counteract any residual acid in the stomach and also helps to re-colonise the natural bacteria.

The honey is anti-inflammatory and antibiotic as well as providing natural sugar in a highly digestible form.

The banana gives calories to get your strength back, also has antibiotic properties and is high in magnesium which is useful in the treatment of diarrhoea.

PHLEGM IN THE THROAT OR SINUSES

As detailed for a sore throat but use an equivalent amount of thyme which is a very effective anti-mucolytic.

COUGH MEDICINE

Chop 1 medium onion very finely and place in a small bowl.
Pour 2 tablespoons of honey over the top.
Cover and leave overnight.
Strain off the juice and take a dessertspoonful every hour or two until the cough is easing.

BRINGING OUT THE FEVER OF COLDS AND FLU

Obviously, I only recommend putting the whisky in for teenagers and adults. And use your common sense, choosing a painkiller that suits you, don't exceed the stated dose etc.

Put into a tall glass:
1 bulging tablespoon of honey.
1 tablespoon of lemon juice.
1 tablespoon of whisky.
Top up the glass with very hot water and stir well until the honey has dissolved.
Drink it all before it goes cold.
Take 2 paracetamol or ibuprofen.
If there is any fever lurking around, this will bring it out and usually guarantees a good night's sleep at the end of it.

HEADACHES – Headaches can be caused by a number of things and if you continually get headaches, it really is a good idea to have a chat with a doctor. Stress or allergies are often major factors, and you should keep notes about what has been happening when your headachs come on. Remember that excessive use of painkillers can actually *exacerbate* headaches, so do be sensible and moderate w ith their use. But these things can help:

HEAT – Lie down in a dark room with a hot water bottle on the back of your neck

PRESSURE POINTS – Put your middle fingers to your temples. Now press your index fingers down next to them and you will find another 'hollow' which is a pressure point. Gently putting pressure on this spot can help to relieve pressure and tension.

CHOCOLATE – For those for whom chocolate is not a cause of migraine in itself, a few pieces of good chocolate can provide some relief.

COLD REMEDIES – If you run out of painkillers, remember that cold and flu remedies have 1,000mg of paracetamol or ibuprofen as well as decongestants that can be very helpful.

ONIONS – An onion poultice can be surprisingly helpful. Boil a large onion, put it through a blender then run it through a muslin to get rid of excess moisture. (Keep the onion liquid for cough syrup). Leave to cool. Place on a muslin, fold up and apply to your head.

VINEGAR —A handkerchief soaked in vinegar, rung out, folded in three and applied to the head is a very old and efficacious remedy. Do make sure that the vinegar can't drip into your eyes.
ELDER – For a nervous headache, hot elder leaves will help. Place a handful of fresh green elder leaves between two plates and heat in the microwave for about 30 seconds or until hot. Put the leaves on your head until they go cold.

THRUSH TREATMENT FOR LADIES OR GENTLEMEN

Firstly, make sure that you keep your bits and pieces very clean indeed and wash with a non-fragranced soap. Wear cotton underwear.

Then thoroughly mix:
1 tablespoon of zinc and castor oil cream with
1 drop tea tree oil

For women – apply gently to the external area. Put some of the cream (¼ teaspoon) onto the end of a tampon, pop it in as usual and leave for a couple of hours, then do it again.
For men – apply gently to the whole end of your willy, making sure you get it under your foreskin where micro-organisms roam free.
Both – Keep treating until symptoms subside. If it doesn't clear up within about 48 hours, talk to your doctor or pharmacist.

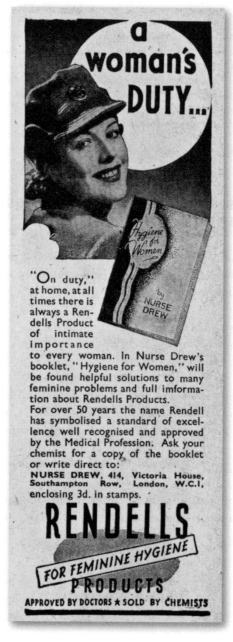

Feminine
hygiene

THE GENTLEMAN'S AREA

Apart from your own joy of hygiene, no one is going to want to rummage around down there if your exhibits are noisesome or unwholesome. Always make sure that you wash thoroughly under the foreskin and encourage boy children to get used to doing this from an early age, not only for hygiene but also to avoid tight foreskins which can be painful.

Masculine
hygiene

Remember that testicles that have been scrunched up in pants and trousers all day need to feel the wind in their hair and, being of a wrinkly disposition, need to be washed just as thoroughly as well. Lying in the bath is a good time to check your balls for any lumps or bumps that are not usually there.

If you get any smelly discharge or inflammation, you must go to your doctor and get it checked out. Doctors have seen a great many knobs in their time and will not be remotely put off by yours. Unless of course you've gone in for a sore throat or an ingrowing toenail.

A Soothing Solution for your Gentleman's Area

1 pint of pleasantly warm water
1 teaspoon vodka
2 drops lavender essential oil
1 teaspoon sea salt

Dissolve the essential oil in the vodka and add to the warm water with the salt. Swish well to dissolve the salt and wash your genital area with it thoroughly. If you have any inflammation, e.g. after sex, put the ingredients into a shallow bowl and let your penis have a good old soak for 10 minutes.

TROUBLE WAKING UP?

Put a few drops of grapefruit essential oil somewhere near your head, i.e. behind your ears or on your collar. Grapefruit is a brain stimulant and will help to get you going.

TROUBLE GOING TO SLEEP?

Have a warm bath into which you have added 10 drops of lavender and 5 drops of chamomile essential oil. Turn down the lights and soak.

Make a lovely mug of Ovaltine or Horlicks and sip it in bed whilst reading something light and unchallenging. This way, if you feel sleepy, you can simply snuggle down and nod off.

If you wake up in the night, don't immediately start fretting about not being asleep. Get up, make yourself a warm drink, go to the loo, go back to bed and read or listen to the radio. Television is too stimulating and the programmes that are on in the middle of the night will probably encourage you to gamble, which will really give you something to worry about.

Herbal preparations such as Kalms and Natrasleep are unexpectedly effective.

SIMPLE CALISTHENICS TO KEEP YOU FIT AND SUPPLE

Simple exercises can be done at any time of the day which can strengthen and firm up your muscles. And you don't need an empty room with a wall of mirrors either – these moves can be done in any space that is as long as your legs. The song 'One Day Like This' by Elbow, or 'The Liberty Bell March' by J. P. Sousa are the right tempo for the first and last. A slowish waltz is needed for the balance exercise such as Johann Strauss' 'The Blue Danube'.

Upper Body
- Stand with your feet apart – about the width of your hips, knees soft. Shoulders in line with hips, but relaxed.
- Put your arms straight out in front of you, in line with your shoulders, hands touching.

Exercise for Nerve Control.

Swimming Exercise (1st position).

Stretching Exercise.

From *The Book of the Home*; 1925. I would very much like one of those gym outfits

- Move your arms, still in line with your shoulders, straight out to the sides.
- Bending at the elbows, bring your hands in to touch your chest, palms down.
- Take your hands back so your arms are outstretched again.
- Arms by your sides and begin a full circle with your arms – out in front, straight up in the air, as far back as they'll go, and bring them to rest straight out in front of you again.
- Repeat.
- Now simultaneously lunge your right foot and knee diagonally to the right whilst stretching your right arm straight in line with your thigh.
- Bring them back, touch your fingertips to your shoulders.
- Put your arms out to your sides at a twenty to four position.
- Clap your hands in front of your chest and return your arms to your sides.
- Repeat the lunge to the left side.
- Bring them back, touch your fingertips to your shoulders.
- Put your arms out to your sides at a twenty to four position.
- Clap your hands in front of your chest and return your arms to your sides.
- Repeat the whole sequence up to four times.

Balance
- Feet together, arms outstretched in line with your shoulders.
- Crouch down with one foot tucked slightly behind the other, arms still out.
- Bring your arms down to a twenty to four position.
- Return to standing and as you do so touch your shoulders, clap your hands in front of your chest and return your hands to your sides.

- Feet together, arms outstretched in line with your shoulders.
- Arms above your head, wrists crossed.
- Arms straight at a ten to two position.
- Clap your hands in front of your chest, touch your shoulders and return your hands to your sides.
- Feet together, arms outstretched in line with your shoulders.
- Crouch down with one foot tucked slightly behind the other, arms still out.
- Bring your arms down to a twenty to four position.
- Return to standing and as you do so touch your shoulders, clap your hands in front of your chest and return your hands to your sides.
- Repeat the whole sequence up to four times.

Legs, Bottom and Lower Back

- Sit on the floor with your legs straight out in front but in line with your hips.
- Put your hands neatly on the floor, palms down at your sides.
- Keeping your left hand on the floor, stretch forward and touch your left toe with your right hand.
- Return your hands to the floor at your sides.
- Keeping your right hand on the floor, stretch forward and touch your right toe with your left hand.
- Sit back up straight and clap both hands on the floor then clap both hands above your head twice.
- Repeat four times.

SWOLLEN FEET AND ANKLES

Feet and ankles can swell up for a variety of reasons such as high blood pressure, fluid retention and congestive ailments such as constipation. Assuming that you've consulted your doctor as to the causes, the first and most effective treatment is to rest with your feet up. A soothing foot bath can also be efficacious:

- Place a few smooth stones into a bowl of warm water.
- Add 1 drop of lavender, 2 drops of cyprus and 2 drops of fennel essential oils to the water.
- Roll your feet gently over the pebbles.

If you can reach or can get someone else to do it for you:

- Mix the same quantity of essential oil with a tablespoon of olive or sweet almond oil.
- Massage your feet, ankles, calves and knees in an upward motion, firmly with the flat of your hands for 5 or 10 minutes.

NATURAL RINSES FOR HEALTHY HAIR

Even though shop-bought preparations promise the earth and often feel lovely at the time, continued use, particularly of conditioners, can start a vicious circle of the more you use the more you need. Herbs and essential oils can be used cheaply and effectively for home beauty treatments tailored for your specific needs.

Greasy Hair
1 tablespoon of rosemary
1 tablespoon mint
2 drops lavender essential oil
1 tablespoon lemon juice
½ pint/300ml hot water

Put everything into a jug, cover and leave for 20 minutes. Strain and rinse the hair with the liquid after washing.

Grey Hair and Problem Scalps

2 pints/1¼ litres of fresh nettle tops
1 tablespoon fresh sage
1 tablespoon rosemary
1 tablespoon cider vinegar

Add the ingredients to a pan with half a pint of water and bring to the boil.
Remove from the heat and leave to infuse for 20 minutes.
Strain and rinse your hair with the liquid.

Dry Hair

1 teaspoon cider vinegar
3 drops of chamomile essential oil
½ teaspoon borax (available from chemists)

Mix the ingredients into a ⅓ pint of boiled water.
Leave to cool and use as the final rinse.

Normal Hair

2 teaspoons cider vinegar
1 teaspoon lemon juice
2 floz/60ml bitter beer
1 drop rosemary oil

Mix together with 2floz/60ml water and use as a rinse.
Leave on for a few minutes then rinse again with cold water.

Limp, Lifeless Hair

1 tablespoon fresh rosemary
2 tablespoons beer
2 tablespoons lemon juice
4 drops calendula essential oil

Place the rosemary, beer and lemon juice in a jug with ⅓ pint/200ml of hot water.

Leave to infuse for 15 minutes.
Add the calendula and use as a final rinse.

Other Hair Treatments

Protein Pack
½ oz/15g gelatin
⅓ pint of water
3 drops clary sage essential oil
3 drops carrot or borage essential oil
1 teaspoon cider vinegar

Mix the gelatine and water together until completely dissolved, then leave to form a gel but not completely set.
Add the other ingredients and mix well.
Apply as a pack to the hair and leave for 10 minutes.
Rinse thoroughly.

Dry Shampoo
1oz/30g pure talc (available from chemists)
10 drops lemon essential oil
2 drops rosemary essential oil

Put the ingredients into a blender or mini chopper and put the lid on tightly!
Mix thoroughly.
Put about a teaspoonful into the roots of your hair and massage well into the roots and lengths.
Brush out.

Beard Conditioner
If you grow a beard, it is essential to keep it clean and fresh; there are few things more off-putting than a chin-full of toast crumbs or curry dregs or a musty smell, under which spots and dry patches can easily form.

2 tablespoons almond oil
1 tablespoon jojoba oil
6 drops lavender essential oil
6 drops cypress essential oil
8 drops lavender essential oil
8 drops rosemary essential oil

Massage a couple of teaspoonfuls, a little at a time so it doesn't drip everywhere, into your beard and skin before you have your bath or shower.
Leave it to soak in whilst you relax then rinse it off with cold water.

Bespoke Aftershave Lotion

Having to shave your face every day is a bother and can be very harsh on your skin, removing its protective layer and leaving the pores open and sensitive as well as being vulnerable to bacteria. You can experiment with the essential oils in this lotion to create your own personal scent, but always keep in the lavender or lemon as they are antibacterial and antiseptic in case of any cuts or rash.

2 tablespoons witch hazel
4 tablespoons rosewater
1 tablespoon cider vinegar
6 drops of lavender essential oil
6 drops lemon essential oil
4 drops lime essential oil
6 drops rosemary essential oil

Put all the ingredients into a bottle with a firm cap or cork and shake well to blend.
Shake the bottle vigorously before each use.

CARE FOR YOUR HANDS

Sea Salt Hand Scrub

This hand scrub is so easy to make, very cheap and makes your hands feel like silk. You will also be startled by how much dirt comes off your hands. I used lavender oil to make it smell lovely, but you could use whatever you like: rose, bergamot, peppermint, ginger etc., and blended it with sea salt and olive oil. Of course you could also use it on your feet, and peppermint oil is wonderfully cooling and refreshing for tired feet.

Just before Christmas someone on a stand at the shopping centre tried to sell me a jar of what was, ostensibly, the recipe below, except the salt came from the Dead Sea. His cost forty quid. Mmmm.

2 heaped tablespoons of coarse sea salt
2–3 tablespoons of olive oil (wheatgerm or sweet almond oil could also be used)
1–2 drops essential oil of your choice

Put the ingredients into a bowl and stir well.
Scoop some onto your hands – a few teaspoonfuls should do it.
Rub it all over your hands, in between the fingers, rub it into your cuticles etc.
Keep going until the salt has all but dissolved.
Wash the excess oil off with a little gentle soap.
Dry your hands – they will feel like silk.
Apply your favourite hand cream.
Keep in a sealed jar.

A Luxurious Hand Cream

For a good jarful:
4 tablespoons almond or peach kernel oil
1 tablespoon beeswax

1 tablespoon cocoa butter
5 drops rose essential oil
5 drops evening primrose essential oil
3 drops geranium essential oil

Place a heatproof bowl over a pan of hot water.
Place the beeswax and cocoa butter in and stir until well mixed.
Remove from the heat and stir in the other oils.
Store in a sealed jar.

Making the Most of Hand Cream

As an extra treat for your hands, buy a pair of cotton gloves
from the chemist. Put your hand cream on, a little more thickly
than usual, then pop on the gloves and go to bed or put your
feet up for an hour. The heat from your hands helps the cream
to be deeply absorbed and more effective.

To Prevent Chapped Hands

Keep a large jar of oatmeal beside the sink. After drying
your hands, plunge them into the oatmeal and rub well into
the skin.

ANTISEPTIC AND ANTI-VIRAL SPRAY FOR LURGY-INFESTED ENVIRONMENTS

How often do we hear, 'Ooh there's a lot of it about!'. Well
I'm sure you don't want it, whatever it is. Apart from normal
hand washing you can help to prevent the spread of infection
by using the following spray. Not only will it kill germs but
it will also keep everyone awake, which is jolly useful in the
work place. Try sprinkling a few drops around the boardroom
before a potentially dull meeting – it works wonders! If
you can't get grapefruit, lemon oil is a reasonable substitute.

1 plant spray
½ pint/300ml water
10 drops grapefruit essential oil

Mix it all together in the sprayer then spray it liberally around the room.

Skin Care

An ancient cure for pimples: Stare into the sky on a clear night and watch for a shooting star. As the star descends towards earth, wipe your pimples with a cloth and throw it to the ground. As the star falls, the pimples will drop off your face. Be very careful not to wipe you face with your hands or the spots will simply transfer to your hands. Except they won't because if it was as easy as this I would have had a significantly better sex life as an adolescent.

Let us progress with all haste to the proper stuff ...

I am a great believer in real faces. I love to see a face with character and laugh lines and the odd scar or blemish to show that people have lived a life. I am as suspicious of an unblemished face as I am of an unblemished character. Now don't get me wrong, I wear enough make up to keep the cosmetics industry alive and kicking for generations, but it's more about accentuating what I have than hiding the ravages of time. I am a pale girl with pig's eyelashes and blonde eyebrows. If I didn't paint some features on, I would probably be run over on zebra crossings.

Lifestyle also takes its toll on our bodies; smoking, drinking, sunbathing, stress, dehydration, poor diet, pollution, hormones – these all take their toll and my approach is to adopt a gentle and natural approach to helping your skin to be the best it can be. And remember that it's not just about what you look like, it's what you *feel* like that really counts.

Also, may I just point out that the boys deserve a bit of looking after in this department as well. There is nothing poncey about looking after your skin and you will be so much nicer to snuggle up to if you are reasonably well-groomed and fragrant.

A Simple Cleanser/Make-up Remover

2oz/60g almond oil

3oz/90g ground almonds

1oz/30g cider vinegar

1oz/30g distilled or spring water

6 drops neroli or rose essential oil

Whisk all the ingredients together in a blender until it becomes a smooth paste.

Store in a tight-lidded jar.

Apply the cleanser gently with your fingertips then wipe off with damp cotton wool.

A Refreshing and Stimulating Astringent Lotion

1oz/30g Witch hazel

3floz/90ml rose water (available from chemists or you can make your own – see below)

1 teaspoon cider vinegar

1 drop peppermint essential oil

1 drop basil essential oil

1 drop chamomile essential oil

Mix all the ingredients together and shake well.

Store in a bottle with a firm lid or cork.

Apply to your skin with damp cotton wool.

A Rather Lovely Face Scrub

Face masks take the dead skin cells off your face and unblock pores, which immediately makes it look dewier and more vibrant. A lot of things in your store cupboard can be pressed into service, so make use of what you have – oatmeal is particularly good for this.

2 teaspoons of ground almonds
2 teaspoons oats
½ teaspoon sea salt
1 teaspoon cider vinegar
1 drop basil essential oil
1 drop rose essential oil

Mix the basil, rose, salt and vinegar together then add the almonds and oats.

Wet your fingers and gently massage the mixture over your face in small circular motions, making sure you include your jaw line and neck.

Rinse off and relax for half an hour with a cup of tea and a good book.

Facial steamers

Facial steamers are also marvellous for your skin, pores, sinuses and your voice. You don't need to buy an expensive electric sauna, a bowl of hot water and a towel will do the job just as well and you can add a drop of your favourite essential oil to the water to boost its efficacy.

• Peppermint or eucalyptus will cleanse and purify as well as unblock your nose
• Lavender will relax and purify
• Grapefruit is astringent and will buck you up a bit
• Rose will lift the spirits and sooth anxiety

Blackheads

Don't you just hate them, particularly when you keep your face nice and clean and they still persist. Blackheads need to be removed as they block the pores and can set up spots or infections.

As a first line of attack, give your face a good steam then rinse your face with some hot water into which you have put a teaspoon of cider vinegar. Gently squeeze any obviously loose blackheads then splash your face with the following:

4floz/125ml distilled or spring water

2 teaspoons cider vinegar

4 drops bergamot essential oil

2 drops grapefruit essential oil

Mix together thoroughly and store in a bottle with a tight lid or cork.

If your blackheads are bad, do this a couple of times a week.

Spots

Tea tree oil can be applied directly to the spots with your fingertip, making sure not to get it near your eyes and to wash your hands thoroughly afterwards.

Lip Balm

2oz/60g light beeswax

4floz/125ml sweet almond oil

10 drops wheatgerm oil

1 drop chamomile essential oil

1 drop calendula essential oil

Put the beeswax and oil into a bowl over a pan of hot water. Melt together, stirring all the time.

Add the other ingredients and store in a jar with a well fitting lid.

Basic Body Cream

You can buy plain, unperfumed lotion to which you can add essential oils of your choice, but this heavy, basic cream will soak into your skin and leave it feeling gorgeous.

1oz/30g light beeswax

2oz/60g cocoa butter

5 tablespoons sweet almond oil

10 drops evening primrose oil
10 drops calendula essential oil
10 drops rose essential oil *or* 5 drops patchouli or sandalwood
for a more masculine smell

Put the beeswax and oil into a bowl over a pan of hot water.
Melt together, stirring all the time.
Add the other ingredients, adding a little more sweet almond
oil if you want it a bit lighter.
Apply as necessary to your skin, massaging well to improve
circulation.

Refreshing Foot Cream

½oz/15g light beeswax
2oz/60g cocoa butter
5 tablespoons sweet almond oil
10 drops peppermint essential oil
2 drops tea tree essential oil
2 drops geranium essential oil

Wash your feet well, and use a pumice stone to smooth away
dead and hard skin.
Dry thoroughly and massage the cream in well, taking care to
get between the toes and into the nail bed.

DISTILL YOUR OWN ROSE WATER

Rose water can be used both as a perfume, a cosmetic (as an
astringent, particularly for fair and dry skin) and a flavouring
for puddings and sweets; who can resist rose flavoured Turkish
delight with its thick coating of icing sugar? And why not try a
teaspoon in a homemade rice pudding?

Utensils

1 large cooking pot with a rounded lid – large enough for a brick
1 slightly smaller bowl
1 house brick

Ingredients

4 pints rose petals
Water
2–3 trays of ice cubes

Method

Put the brick into the cooking pot, then put the bowl on the brick.

Put the rose petals into the pot (around the brick).

Top up the pot with water to about level with the top of the brick.

Place the lid upside down over the top of the bowl and the pot making sure that the handle in the middle of the lid is right over the bowl.

Put the pot on the stove and heat and bring to the boil.

As soon as it boils, put the ice cubes on top of the lid.

Immediately turn down the heat and let it simmer.

The steam will then start to condense and drip into the bowl.

After about 20 minutes lift the lid quickly and take a teaspoon of the liquid. When it begins to taste and smell strongly of roses remove the bowl from the heat. It should only take about 40 minutes.

Pour the rosewater into sterilized bottles and store in a cool place.

BABIES

Babies' skins are so delicate and perfect that it seems an affront to put chemicals or perfumes on them. Wipes and creams can be made at home, naturally and with minimum effort and without filling the landfill sites with waste that takes years to biodegrade. It goes without saying that I am in favour of using terry nappies. Not only do they cost less and mean an astonishing amount less going to landfill, but when your children get older they have a whole other life as cleaning cloths, mop-ups, mattress liners for the bedwetters etc. You can get more information about them here: www.which.co.uk/baby-and-child/nursery-and-feeding/guides/choosing-nappies-washable-vs-disposable/washable-nappies.

Make Your Own Baby Wipes

Cut up old towels into lots of small squares that will fit in a large, sealable Tupperware box.

Put ½–1 pint (3–600ml) of cool boiled water into a jug.

Add 5 drops of lavender and 5 drops of chamomile essential oils.

Stir well and pour over the cloths.

Seal the tub for use throughout the day.

Put the used cloths into the nappy bucket for washing.

Nappy Rash

Put warm water into a small bowl and add 1 drop of lavender and 1 drop of chamomile essential oil to the water.

Dip cotton wool into the water and bathe the affected area.

Baby Cream

2 tablespoons of zinc and castor oil cream

2 drops of lavender essential oil

2 drops of chamomile essential oil

Mix all the ingredients together well.

Place in a sealed container and use at each nappy change.

Cradle Cap

Cradle cap is very common in babies and is a brown crusty accumulation on the scalp which does no harm but is unsightly. It is caused by excess sebum combined with fast growing skin so you need something gentle to break down the oil and stop it coming back. Never use lavender oil as this will make it worse.

Mix 1 tablespoon olive oil with 2 drops of eucalyptus and blend well.

Gently massage this into the scalp using your fingertips, taking great care to avoid the soft part at the front of the baby's head called the fontanelle.

Do this daily until the cradle cap has gone.
The crusts will drop off and not come back.

Sleeping

A couple of drops of lavender on the cot sheet or in the bath water will help to promote deep sleep and relaxation for your baby.

PETS

I could write a whole book on pets but I thought I'd pop this in here because animals can benefit from a more natural approach to health, and medicines from vets can be horrifically expensive.

Cat bites are really horrible and they will usually attempt to bite each other in places that they can't lick clean, the back of the neck and the topside of the base of the tail being favourite targets. If you suspect your cat of being in a fight, always check its tail, as a bite can quickly turn into an abscess which, if left untreated could result in an amputated tail. Hey presto! One Manx cat you haven't bargained for.

If your cat has a cut or graze, mix 1 drop of thyme essential oil with ¼ pint /150ml of cool, boiled water. Using clean cotton wool, bathe the area with the thyme water until it looks clean.

If you can see the beginnings of an abscess, apply 1 drop of neat tea tree oil onto it to bring it to a head. If the cat can reach, it will ingest the oil which will also help the healing process. Keep doing this daily until it bursts. When it does, mix 1 drop lavender oil with 1 tablespoon cool boiled water and bathe the area a couple of times a day to keep it clean, bacteria free and to promote healing.

The same remedies apply to dogs, but you will need to increase the quantities:

- A cat-sized dog can be treated as opposite.
- A medium-sized dog, e.g. spaniel, use 2 drops thyme to ¼ pint/150ml cool boiled water.
- A large-sized dog, e.g. German Shepherd, use 3 drops thyme to ¼ pint /150ml cool boiled water.
- A giant-sized dog, e.g. Great Dane, use 4 drops thyme to ¼ pint /150ml cool boiled water.

The area can then be kept clean with the lavender and water as you need it.

- Thyme, tea tree and lavender are heavy duty anti-bacterial agents and they are also antiseptic, antiviral and antifungal.
- Lavender is a cictrizant (i.e. it promotes healing) and it is calming to animals and humans alike.
- Thyme is particularly effective for the treatment of wounds and sores and acts as a stimulant to the immune system.
- Tea tree helps to soothe inflammation and is effective at treating shock.

Remember – *If you are in any doubt about your pet's health, be sensible and consult your vet first.*

CONCLUSION

So what conclusion can be drawn from a thorough reading of this No-Nonsense Handbook? What can be said to sum up the contents of this book that I didn't cover in my introduction? This is the point where you all flick manically back to the beginning to see what witticisms and extreme sageness you missed by being too idle to read the introduction. Although, on second thought, I did suggest that you open the book at random and choose something to do, so I have no one to blame but myself.

I have the overwhelming temptation to launch into a contemporary domestic equivalent of the Beatitudes and encourage you all to love one another, don't upset anyone, eat broccoli, walk about a bit and generally do more baking. But that might be a *bit* presumptuous, and as I know to my cost, the police in Market Harborough take an awfully dim view of people shouting in the market square about how blessed are the cake-makers and so forth. The magistrates were very understanding but made it clear that if I do it again …

I suppose the crux of the matter is that we must all do our best and have the courage of our convictions. At one point during the writing of this book, the boys and I ate nothing but crap and convenience food for a week, and they were rotating their underpants and not daring to remove their jumpers at school because I was working eighteen-hour days and had no time for anything. I was just about to start beating myself up when Boy the Elder reminded me that I was not Superwoman and that a week of abject neglect was not necessarily a matter for the social services.

And he was right. The Wartime Housewife is not about lecturing or making people feel inadequate; it's about empowerment and fun, gentle encouragement towards a more natural and sustainable way of living, a rallying cry against the joyless tide of infantilism and interference by those who have no business telling us how to live. As they say in the Scouts, "Do your best." To which you reply, "Yes, WH, we *will* do our best!"

Now, stop reading this conclusion and make yourself a nice hot cup of tea (an accompanying Bath bun is entirely possible now that I have taught you how to make them). Look at yourself in the mirror and say, "You're fab! I <u>like</u> you." Brush the crumbs off your pullover and go and do something lovely. You won't regret it.

With love and best wishes

Wartime Housewife

INDEX